Culturally Relevant Teaching in the English Language Arts Classroom

This book is a practical, research-based, classroom-ready resource for English language arts teachers interested in learning how to incorporate culturally relevant pedagogy into all aspects of their instruction, including writing, reading, and vocabulary lessons. It also provides suggestions for building an inclusive classroom environment in which all students' backgrounds are valued.

Topics covered:

- Writing strategies and diverse texts
- Dialect and student writing
- Applying reading strategies to texts that represent diverse backgrounds
- Using reading strategies in out-of-school contexts
- Considering students' funds of knowledge and language awareness
- Connecting linguistic diversity to word-root instruction
- Building an inclusive classroom environment

The appendix features several useful tools, including a study guide, a comprehensive list of suggested texts, recommendations for parent communication, and reproducible tools for the classroom. The study guide and reproducibles are available for free download from our website at www.routledge.com/9781138393318.

Sean Ruday is an associate professor of English Education at Longwood University and a former classroom teacher. He frequently writes and presents on innovative ways to improve students' literacy learning. He is the author of eight other books, including *The First-Year English Teacher's Guidebook* and *The Common Core Grammar Toolkit* series for grades 3–5, 6–8, and 9–12.

Also Available from Sean Ruday

The First-Year English Teacher's Guidebook
Strategies for Success

The Common Core Grammar Toolkit
Using Mentor Texts to Teach the Language Standards in Grades 3–5

The Common Core Grammar Toolkit
Using Mentor Texts to Teach the Language Standards in Grades 3–5

The Common Core Grammar Toolkit
Using Mentor Texts to Teach the Language Standards in Grades 9–12

The Multimedia Writing Toolkit
Helping Students Incorporate Graphics and Videos for Authentic Purposes, Grades 3–8

The Informational Writing Toolkit
Using Mentor Texts in Grades 3–5

The Argument Writing Toolkit
Using Mentor Texts in Grades 6–8

The Narrative Writing Toolkit
Using Mentor Texts in Grades 3–8

Culturally Relevant Teaching in the English Language Arts Classroom

A Guide for Teachers

Sean Ruday

Routledge
Taylor & Francis Group

NEW YORK AND LONDON

First published 2019
by Routledge
52 Vanderbilt Avenue, New York, NY 10017

and by Routledge
2 Park Square, Milton Park, Abingdon, Oxon, OX14 4RN

Routledge is an imprint of the Taylor & Francis Group, an informa business

© 2019 Taylor & Francis

The right of Sean Ruday to be identified as author of this work has been asserted by him in accordance with sections 77 and 78 of the Copyright, Designs and Patents Act 1988.

All rights reserved. The purchase of this copyright material confers the right on the purchasing institution to photocopy or download pages which bear the eResources icon and a copyright line at the bottom of the page. No other parts of this book may be reprinted or reproduced or utilised in any form or by any electronic, mechanical, or other means, now known or hereafter invented, including photocopying and recording, or in any information storage or retrieval system, without permission in writing from the publishers.

Trademark notice: Product or corporate names may be trademarks or registered trademarks, and are used only for identification and explanation without intent to infringe.

Library of Congress Cataloging-in-Publication Data
Names: Ruday, Sean, author.
Title: Culturally relevant teaching in the English language arts classroom : a guide for teachers / Sean Ruday.
Description: New York, NY : Routledge, 2019. | Includes bibliographical references.
Identifiers: LCCN 2018034652 (print) | LCCN 2018052257 (ebook) | ISBN 9780429401831 (ebook) | ISBN 9781138317710 (hardback) | ISBN 9781138393318 (pbk.).
Subjects: LCSH: English language—Study and teaching—Social aspects. | Culturally relevant pedagogy. | Multicultural education. | Classroom environment.
Classification: LCC LB1576 (ebook) | LCC LB1576 .R7765 2019 (print) | DDC 372.6—dc23
LC record available at https://lccn.loc.gov/2018034652

ISBN: 978-1-138-31771-0 (hbk)
ISBN: 978-1-138-39331-8 (pbk)
ISBN: 978-0-429-40183-1 (ebk)

Typeset in Palatino and Formata
by Apex CoVantage, LLC

Visit the eResources: http://www.routledge.com/9781138393318

Contents

Meet the Author vii
Acknowledgements vii
eResources ix

Introduction: What is Culturally Relevant Teaching and
Why is it Important? 1

Section 1: Culturally Relevant Writing Instruction 9
  1 Writing Strategies and Diverse Texts 11
  2 Dialect and Student Writing 29

Section 2: Culturally Relevant Reading Instruction 47
  3 Applying Reading Strategies to Texts that Represent
     Diverse Backgrounds 49
  4 Using Reading Strategies in Out-of-School Contexts 71

Section 3: Culturally Relevant Language Study 91
  5 Considering Students' Funds of Knowledge and
     Language Awareness 93
  6 Connecting Linguistic Diversity to Word-Root Instruction 105

Section 4: Putting It All Together 115
  7 Ideas for Building an Inclusive Classroom Environment 117
  8 Recommendations for Putting this Book's Ideas
     into Action 123

Section 5: Resources 127

  Appendix A: A Guide for Book Studies 129
  Appendix B: Reproducible Forms and Templates You Can
    Use in Your Classroom 133

Appendix C: Classroom Library Recommendations—
   Multicultural Texts 149
Appendix D: Recommendations for Parent Communication 151
References 153

Meet the Author

Sean Ruday is an Associate Professor of English Education at Longwood University. He began his teaching career at a public school in Brooklyn, NY, and has taught English and language arts in New York, Massachusetts, and Virginia. Sean is a Co-President of the Assembly for the Teaching of English Grammar—a grammar-focused affiliate of the National Council of Teachers of English. He is the founder and editor of the *Journal of Literacy Innovation*. Some publications in which his articles have appeared are *Journal of Teaching Writing, Journal of Language and Literacy Education, Contemporary Issues in Technology and Teacher Education,* and the *Yearbook of the Literacy Research Association*. His professional website is seanruday.weebly.com. You can follow him on Twitter @SeanRuday. This is his ninth book with Routledge Eye on Education.

Acknowledgements

I am filled with gratitude for the fantastic individuals who helped make this book possible:

- The wonderful teachers who shared their thoughts and gave me the opportunity to work with them and their students.
- The amazing students whose ideas, insights, and writings are included in this book.
- This book's editor, Lauren Davis, whose support and guidance have been integral to my work as a writer.
- My parents, Bob and Joyce Ruday, for encouraging me to pursue my dream of becoming a teacher.
- My wife, Clare Ruday, who brightens my life by bringing humor and happiness to it.

eResources

Appendices A and B of this book can also be downloaded and printed for classroom use. You can access these downloads by visiting the book product page on our website: http://www.routledge.com/9781138393318. Then click on the tab that says "eResources," and select the files. They will begin downloading to your computer.

Introduction

What is Culturally Relevant Teaching and Why is it Important?

I'm standing in front of a group of future English and language arts teachers and am smiling with delight: their comments about the importance of culturally relevant literacy instruction convey their understanding of this significant and nuanced topic.

"This might be the most important thing I've learned about in any of my teacher-education classes," one student explains. "We need to make sure our students' cultures are valued when we teach them."

"And," continues another student, "I think it's so cool that we can actually use our students' cultures to help them learn. I totally never thought about that before."

"Those are wonderful insights," I respond. "Culturally relevant teaching is a fantastic tool for facilitating student success. Today, we talked about what culturally relevant pedagogy is, why it's important, and what it can look like in the ELA classroom. As you begin your teaching careers, I want you to keep culturally relevant teaching at the forefront of your instruction. We teachers don't just teach a subject—we also teach our individual students. To best teach those students, we need to think about who they are and the best ways to help them learn."

This opening vignette provides a snapshot of future teachers beginning to understand the significance of culturally relevant teaching to the success of all students. Many of the pre- and in-service teachers I work with have a general understanding of culturally relevant teaching and believe that making connections to students' home lives and cultures is a good thing, but they aren't aware of exactly what this educational concept is and why it can enhance ELA instruction in elementary, middle, and high school. When I first began teaching, I was like many people I now meet in the education classes I teach and professional development workshops I conduct: I figured bringing students' home cultures into my middle school English instruction was good, but didn't yet know about research-based and classroom-tested practices and ideas that are essential to strong culturally relevant pedagogy.

In this book, we'll consider the components of culturally relevant teaching, drawing on insights from research and practice to discuss what this concept is and to consider the best ways to integrate it into effective English and language arts instruction. This introductory chapter contains four components designed to begin our exploration of culturally relevant teaching and its applications in the ELA classroom:

- The characteristics of culturally relevant teaching
- The importance of culturally relevant teaching
- Why I decided to write this book
- What to expect in this book

The Characteristics of Culturally Relevant Teaching

Culturally relevant teaching is instruction that works to eliminate the feeling of separation between school and community (Tremmel, 2006) by building bridges between students' out-of-school lives and the experiences they have in school. This instructional approach is an effective way to teach English and language arts to students from diverse ethnic backgrounds in academically meaningful ways (Winn & Johnson, 2011): as you'll see in this book, the tactics and ideas described in the book provide students with opportunities to connect strategies they learn in school to aspects of their cultural backgrounds and out-of-school lives. So, how do we build these bridges and make these connections? Gloria Ladson-Billings (1995), a leading scholar on this topic, explains that culturally relevant teaching should achieve three goals: 1) Facilitate students' academic success, 2) Value students' home cultures, and 3) Help students think critically about the world around them. Let's look closely at each of the goals and reflect on what they mean.

Culturally Relevant Teaching Should Facilitate Students' Academic Success

At first glance, this goal might seem somewhat obvious (shouldn't all teaching facilitate students' academic success?), but a deeper look reveals its complexity and nuance: some educational practices that make connections to students' out-of-school lives and cultures are only done so to "hook" or engage students and don't provide much educational value, while other practices not only connect to students' interests and cultures, but also use them as ways to facilitate learning. I recently explained this distinction to a new teacher I was mentoring by using the example of incorporating popular music into English instruction: "If you play a popular song at the beginning of class because your students like it and you think it will get them excited about being at school, but then don't do anything else with that song, you're not really using it as a way to promote learning. However, if you encourage students to bring in songs that represent their interests and backgrounds and work with them to analyze how the writers of those songs use the writing strategies you're discussing in class, then you're using students' interests and cultures to facilitate their understandings of academic topics."

I urge teachers who incorporate students' backgrounds and cultures into their instruction to be sure they can identify the specific academic goal those cultural aspects are being used to achieve and exactly how they contribute to the goal's achievement. If articulating these relationships is difficult, it's probably best to revise the instructional practice so that the cultural component is clearly aligned with helping students master academic content. In this book, we'll explore a number of culturally relevant instructional practices that are designed to facilitate students' academic success in relevant ways, such as the use of dialect to enhance student writing, the application of reading strategies of texts that represent diverse backgrounds, and the analysis of the language used in students' out-of-school lives.

Culturally Relevant Teaching Should Value Students' Home Cultures
In addition to facilitating academic achievement, successful culturally relevant teaching also values students' home backgrounds and cultures. This instructional approach views students' cultures as vehicles for learning (Ladson-Billings, 1995) by looking for ways their cultural backgrounds can be integrated into instruction to help them understand academic material. An example of this is the study of dialect use in literature: a culturally relevant approach to dialect could draw on the different forms of language students use and hear in their lives to help them understand why characters in literature communicate using different linguistic registers. For instance, Paul Fleischman's novel *Seedfolks* (2004) lends itself to valuing students' home dialects and exploring how the use of language variety enhances the effectiveness of the book. *Seedfolks* is told from multiple points of view and each character in the text communicates in a distinctive way, making the book an excellent example of the value of dialect: if every character in this book used the same kind of language, much of the characterization and authenticity in the text would be missing. Discussing *Seedfolks* (and other texts that purposefully and carefully use language variations) helps students understand the importance of the author's choices and values the dialects and linguistic forms associated with their home lives and cultural backgrounds.

Culturally Relevant Teaching Should Help Students Think Critically About the World Around Them
Culturally relevant teaching can also help students analyze the world around them by training them to look carefully at the perspectives and ideas promoted in society and school. For example, students can reflect on what texts are taught in school and why, considering questions like "Whose perspectives are represented in these texts?" "What perspectives are missing?," and "What texts can be adding to address those missing perspectives?" I recently conducted a discussion about this topic with a high-school English class, asking them to work individually at first and

then in small groups to consider what perspectives are present in the texts they read in school, which ones are missing, and which texts they'd recommend. One student asserted, "We've studied authors of different cultures, but it seems like we just read one author from most cultures. I wish we'd read a wider range of different authors from each culture, so we can think more about the differences in each of the authors we study."

Another student concurred: "Yeah, when you only read one author from a certain ethnic background, you only get one person's perspective. If we read more things written by Native American writers, for example, we'd get more perspectives from different people from that culture."

"Those are such thoughtful responses," I replied. "I love how carefully you considered the perspectives that you're exposed to in the books you're assigned, the perspectives to which you're not exposed, and the changes you'd like made."

The work that students did in this activity is an excellent representation of the culture-focused critical thinking that culturally relevant teaching promotes. By asking students to think analytically about the world around them, we facilitate their development as learners and as socially-conscious citizens.

The Importance of Culturally Relevant Teaching

Culturally relevant teaching is important to maximizing the likelihood that all students, especially those from underserved backgrounds, are able to succeed academically (Howard, 2001). Wlodkowski and Ginsberg's (1995) seminal work on this topic identified four reasons that culturally relevant instruction is a key tool to facilitate students' success: 1) It can create an inclusive classroom, 2) It can improve students' attitudes, 3) It can make students' work more meaningful, and 4) It can increase students' feelings of competence.

Culturally Relevant Teaching Can Create an Inclusive Classroom

I think of the inclusiveness that culturally relevant instruction promotes as the key benefit that makes all of the other strengths of this pedagogical approach possible. Valuing students' home cultures is especially important in the English classroom, where many students don't see themselves represented in traditionally taught texts, authors, and topics (Wheeler & Swords, 2006). By creating learning activities in which students' backgrounds, cultures, and home lives are valued, we teachers can create inclusive and welcoming atmospheres in which students see themselves represented in meaningful and important ways. This benefit can be achieved through the use of multicultural texts in our instruction, opportunities for students to connect academic concepts to their home lives and backgrounds, and awareness of students' cultural experiences. The more we value diverse perspectives in our instruction, the greater the likelihood that we create inclusive environments.

Culturally Relevant Teaching Can Improve Students' Attitudes
This benefit of culturally relevant teaching extends from the preceding one: the inclusive atmosphere that culturally relevant teaching creates can enhance students' attitudes toward learning. When students feel their experiences and values are privileged in their ELA instruction, it's likely that they'll have a more positive outlook toward their academic work than they would if their experiences were not represented (Wlodkowski & Ginsberg, 1995). My conversations with students and teachers support these ideas. An eighth grader recently explained that the opportunity to write about high-interest topics improved his disposition toward English class: "This year, we did a lot of research on topics that we were interested in. I got to research safety in football, like which parts of the game have gotten safer and which still need to become safer. This is really interesting to me because my dad, my brothers, and I all played or play football, and because football is such a big deal here in this town and at [the local high school he plans to attend]. I was much more interested in English class and worked a lot harder once I got to work on something I was really interested in." A tenth-grade English teacher noticed an improvement in her students' attitudes when she gave her students opportunities to pair popular songs with poems they studied in class: "All of my students really loved pairing poems we studied with songs they chose that had similar themes. Even the students who didn't seem to usually like English had great attitudes in class and were really engaged when we did this." Both of these examples illustrate ways choice, relevance, and opportunities to connect in-school learning to students' out-of-school lives enhanced students' attitudes toward their English classes.

Culturally Relevant Teaching Can Make Students' Work More Meaningful
Students who are taught in culturally relevant ways are likely to find their academic work more meaningful: these instructional practices increase students' ownership of their learning and their opportunities to see themselves in their academic work (Wlodkowski & Ginsberg, 1995). It's certainly important for students to master important standards in academically rigorous environments, but instruction should also make connections to students' cultures and out-of-school lives at the same time (Duncan-Andrade & Morrell, 2005). By helping our students relate academic topics to their home lives and cultures, we can maximize the sense of personal meaning they find in their learning. For example, in Chapter 4 of this book, I discuss ways that students can apply the close-reading and critical-thinking strategies they learn in the English classroom to their out-of-school lives, such as making connections, creating inferences, and

analyzing word choice to make sense of songs, films, television shows, social media posts, and other texts that are relevant to their lives. These applications provide meaning and authenticity to students' academic work, while still helping them master important academic concepts and strategies.

Culturally Relevant Teaching Can Increase Students' Feelings of Competence

Students who are disengaged from school often feel that way because they see their out-of-school lives as unrelated to what they learn in school (Duncan-Andrade & Morrell, 2005). Culturally relevant teaching can address this issue by conveying to students that their home and school lives aren't distinct and instead can be meaningfully connected. Forging the connection between students' in-school learning and out-of-school lives can help students feel competent in and out-of-school. Students' in-school feelings of competence can increase because they see their home lives as having meaningful connections to the academic material they're asked to learn—a feeling that many students don't have when they don't see their lives, backgrounds, and interests represented in school (Azano, 2011; Wheeler & Swords, 2006). In addition, students' feelings of competence outside of school can increase when they feel that the material they learn in school can help them further make sense of their home lives and communities. The instructional ideas and practices we'll explore together in this book will give you the tools to achieve this important goal with your students, enhancing the value that English class has for them in a variety of contexts.

Why I Decided to Write this Book

I chose to write this book to provide English and language arts teachers in upper-elementary, middle, and high schools with a practical guide to implementing culturally relevant teaching in their classes. While research on this topic has existed for some time (such as the "classic" sources from Ladson-Billings and Wlodkowski & Ginsberg, both published in 1995, cited in this chapter), there is a need for practitioner-oriented texts—written with today's students in mind—that serve as guides for teachers looking to put this important concept into action in their classes. (As I write, there is a thread on the National Council of Teachers of English Connected Community Message Board on this topic that originated with a teacher asking for recommendations on teaching in culturally relevant ways and for texts to guide teachers as they try to do so.)

In addition to helping fill an important need in the practitioner-oriented body of literature, I am also motivated to write this book because of my passion for the topic. I began my career as an English teacher at an urban middle school in Brooklyn, NY and quickly found that culturally relevant teaching is an essential component of effective English instruction. I used song lyrics to help students understand writing strategies, made connections to local dialects to enhance students' awareness of characterization, and helped students use critical-thinking skills to reflect on the importance of community events, such as the annual West Indian Day Parade—a tradition in the neighborhood in which I taught, and where my students lived. These instructional practices gave me first-hand confirmation of what research says about the importance of culturally relevant teaching: making these connections to my students' home lives and communities helped them master academic skills and strategies and see their work in school as related to their out-of-school lives.

What to Expect in This Book

I've designed this book to provide a practical, classroom-ready resource for English and language arts teachers interested in learning how to incorporate culturally relevant pedagogy into all aspects of their instruction. With this goal in mind, the book's first three sections each address an important component of literacy instruction: Section 1 contains two chapters that discuss culturally relevant writing instruction, Section 2 features two chapters on culturally relevant reading instruction, and the two chapters in Section 3 describe ideas for incorporating culturally relevant teaching into language and vocabulary instruction.

For consistency and ease of use, I've organized each chapter in Sections 1 through 3 in a common format:

- "What Is It?" This section provides a description of the instructional method described in the chapter, discussing its key features and why it is an example of culturally relevant teaching.
- "How Can It Help Students?" This part of the chapter explores the benefits of the chapter's focal strategy, explaining how that strategy can help students connect academic content with their out-of-school lives.
- "How Can It Look in Action?" In this section, I describe specific assignments and activities you can use with your students as you put the chapter's focal concept into action.
- "Key Points." This concluding component provides a bulleted list of key ideas discussed in the chapter. It is designed to give you a summary of the chapter's main points and is a useful way to review the chapter's essential information.

Next in the book is Section 4; as its title "Putting it All Together" suggests, this section is designed to help you synthesize the book's main points and reflect on ways to put the book's essential ideas into action in your classroom. The first chapter in this section, Chapter 7, discusses practical ways to use culturally relevant instruction to build an inclusive classroom environment in which all students' backgrounds and out-of-school lives are valued. Next, in Chapter 8, I discuss key recommendations for putting the book's ideas into action—these suggestions will maximize the usefulness of the book and give you a clear plan for implementing culturally relevant teaching in your instruction.

The book concludes with Section 5, which contains resources designed to support you in your work as a culturally relevant teacher. The "Guide for Book Studies" in Appendix A identifies thought-provoking reflection questions and prompts to consider when using this book as a book-study text. I highly recommend engaging in a book study of this text with other teachers in your professional learning network; doing so can allow you to collaboratively discuss the culturally relevant teaching practices the book describes and brainstorm ways to apply its ideas to your own instruction. Appendix B provides reproducible versions of forms and templates featured in this book, maximizing the book's usefulness to your instruction. Appendix C contains recommendations of multicultural texts teachers can include in their classroom libraries (or administrators and librarians can incorporate in school libraries) to ensure that a wide range of cultures and backgrounds are represented in the offerings available to their students. These text-recommendation lists are grouped in three sections: upper-elementary, middle, and high school. Appendix D describes effectively communicating with parents about culturally relevant English language arts instruction; it contains suggestions on how to communicate with parents about what culturally relevant teaching is, how it can benefit their students, and how they can be part of the process. Finally, the reference section provides citation information about many valuable and informative sources that you can examine if you'd like to investigate this topic in more detail.

Culturally relevant teaching is a key tool for maximizing our students' abilities to be successful in school and in life: it values students' backgrounds and uses their out-of-school lives to help them learn academic content. Learning how to be a culturally relevant teacher is one of the most important things any educator can do because of the difference it can make in students' lives and educations; I'm thrilled that you've chosen to make this book your guide in your learning about this essential topic. Now, let's begin our exploration of culturally relevant teaching!

Section 1

Culturally Relevant Writing Instruction

1

Writing Strategies and Diverse Texts

In this chapter, we'll explore the culturally relevant instructional practice of identifying and analyzing writing strategies in a wide range of texts—especially those related to students' cultural backgrounds and out-of-school lives. First, we'll consider it means to help students connect the study of writing strategies to a diverse range of texts, highlighting the main features of this instructional approach. Next, we'll explore the benefits of this instructional practice, addressing ways it can enhances students' academic and personal development. After that, I'll discuss ways this practice can look in action in ELA classes of varying grade levels by presenting three different assignments (designed for elementary, middle, and high school, respectively) that can help students connect writing strategies and diverse texts. Finally, I'll present key points to consider when putting the idea discussed in this chapter into action in your classes.

What Is It?

In this instructional practice, teachers help students understand the wide range of texts to which standards-based and academically rigorous writing strategies can be applied. The tools of effective writing—such as using incorporating sensory details, establishing a clear focus, using specific nouns and strong verbs to communicate information in clear and direct ways, and employing connotation-rich language—aren't limited to the types of writing students traditionally read and create in school; instead, these writing strategies are used in a variety of texts, such as songs, films, and social media posts, sports broadcasts, recipes, and family stories. There are four main components to the process I use when helping students understand how writing strategies can be applied to diverse texts. First, I introduce a strategy with a mini-lesson that illustrates its fundamental components. Next, I talk with students about the impact of that strategy on effective communication, using an example of its use in literature to convey its significance and facilitate a conversation on how it enhances the text in which it's used. Next, I ask students to do some "investigative work" by looking for, identifying, and analyzing relevant examples of the writing strategy they encounter in their out-of-school lives and communities. After that, I schedule time for students to share the culturally relevant examples of the writing strategies they identified and analyzed. Finally, I ask for students to incorporate the strategy in their own writing and reflect on its impact. The specific ways you integrate these components can vary based on the grade level you're teaching and the writing strategy you're addressing; we'll explore grade and strategy-specific lesson ideas and instructional practices later in the chapter.

How Can It Help Students?

This instructional practice can benefit students in a variety of ways: it can give students additional opportunities to apply their understandings of writing strategies; it can help students build confidence in their knowledge of writing strategies through the use of familiar texts, and it can show students that their cultural backgrounds and out-of-school lives belong in school. Let's look at each of these benefits individually.

It Can Give Students Additional Opportunities to Apply Their Understandings

When we encourage our students to look for examples of writing strategies in texts they encounter outside of school, we give them additional opportunities to apply their knowledge: this instructional practice significantly increases the number of possible texts to which students can identify the writing strategies they learn in school. While it's important and beneficial for students to find and analyze examples of writing strategies in published texts they typically encounter in school, encouraging students to identify the uses of key writing strategies in texts they wouldn't typically see in school provides them with more chances to use their skills.

It Can Help Students Build Confidence in Their Knowledge of Writing Strategies

This instructional practice can also use students' familiarity with culturally relevant texts to help them develop confidence in their knowledge writing strategies. By giving students opportunities to look for examples of the writing strategies in texts that represent their out-of-school lives and cultural backgrounds, we create a learning environment that utilizes students' background knowledge to help them understand academic material. I believe that incorporating students' background knowledge in any academic context can enhance their learning by showing them what they already know and developing their confidence to understand a topic even more. For example, after I asked a group of middle-school students to identify prepositional phrases in texts they encountered outside of school, one explained that the practice made an intimidating topic seem manageable: "I looked for prepositional phrases in the lyrics of songs my siblings and I listen to. When we first started talking about [prepositional phrases] in class, I was stressed because I'm not usually good with grammar and writing, but when I looked for examples in songs I know and like, I didn't feel stressed. I was using songs I'm familiar with it, and that made me feel like I could do it. I was sure of myself."

It Can Show Students That Their Cultural Backgrounds and Out-of-School Lives Belong in School

Giving students opportunities to identify examples of writing strategies in culturally relevant texts sends the message that their in-school learning and out-of-school lives can be intertwined. When students are able to apply material that they learn in school to their own lives, they learn to see academic content as relevant to real-world issues and able to help them make sense of their own lives (Duncan-Andrade & Morrell, 2005). I recently prepared a group of middle-school students to look for examples of writing strategies in out-of-school texts by emphasizing the connection between the strategies we studied and their home lives: "The strategies we've been talking about that add detail to writing, like prepositional phrases and relative clauses, aren't just related to school. They can be present in all kinds of texts you find—songs you hear, stories your family members tell, and signs and advertisements you find in your neighborhood. There are so many ways you can find these strategies we learn about here in school in out-of-school situations."

Traditional educational practices sometimes convey to students that they should think one way while they're in school and another while they're out of school (Duncan-Andrade & Morrell, 2005); culturally relevant teaching practices (like students identifying examples of writing strategies in their home lives and communities) communicate that students' out-of-school lives have a place in their in-school learning.

How Can It Look in Action?

In this section, we'll look at three activities that you can use to help your students identify and analyze examples of writing strategies in diverse texts that represent their home cultures and out-of-school lives. These activities are organized by grade level: the first is designed for upper-elementary-school students, the second for middle schoolers, and the third for high-school students. Each activity description provides grade-level-oriented text and content suggestions (although you should feel free to adapt some of the components to meet the particular needs and interests of the specific students with whom you work).

Elementary School: Strong Verbs and Specific Nouns in Community Conversations

In this activity, elementary-school students look for examples of strong verbs and specific nouns in language they hear in conversations in their homes, communities, and activities. The writing strategy of using specific nouns and strong verbs aligns with the Common Core State Standards for elementary school (Common Core Standard L.4.3 calls for students to master this concept), as well as many state standards; this tactic is important to effective writing because of the way it allows for students to express their ideas in clear and concise ways. For example, the strong verb "whisper" clearly conveys how a character made a statement; in contrast, the weaker, or less clear verb "said" does not illustrate the character's action as clearly. An author could add a modifier to the word "said," such as "said quietly," but this usage would be both wordier and less clear than its strong verb replacement. Now, let's look at a step-by-step process for helping elementary-school students understand this concept and apply it in culturally relevant ways.

Step 1: Introduce the Strategy

To begin this activity, conduct a mini-lesson that describes the writing strategies of specific nouns and strong verbs: this will ensure that all students enter the instructional sequence with common understandings of these writing strategies. When I introduce specific nouns and strong verbs to students, I explain what makes a specific noun specific and strong verb strong. After discussing these fundamental features, I like to show students grade-appropriate published examples of each one so that they can see how published authors use these concepts in their works.

Step 2: Explain its Impact

After you've discussed the key features of this strategy and shown students examples, the next step is to talk with the students about its importance. To help students grasp the significance of specific nouns and strong verbs, I suggest taking the published examples you showed them in the previous step, replacing these concepts with vague versions, and talking with students about the differences. For example, in the book *Fantastic Mr. Fox*, author Roald Dahl (1970) uses the strong verb "clutching" in the sentence "Mr. Fox and Badger and the Smallest Fox ran across the cellar clutching a gallon jar each" (p. 71) to clearly convey how an action is performed; if Dahl instead used a weaker, more generic verb like "holding," readers wouldn't have such a clear understanding of how the characters in the book performed the action. In addition, Dahl utilizes specific nouns to make the information in this book as clear as possible; in the sentence "At six o'clock in the evening, Bean switched off the motor of his tractor and climbed down from the driver's seat" (p. 29), the specific noun "tractor" provides the clarity and conciseness that a more general noun could not. For example, a general noun like "vehicle" would not provide the reader with concrete information; even a noun phrase like "farming vehicle" would still lack the clear and direct information that "tractor" provides.

Similarly, Kwame Alexander's (2014) novel *The Crossover* uses strong verbs and specific nouns to clearly convey actions and objects it describes. For example, Alexander utilizes these concepts in the following line, which describes protagonist Josh Bell's basketball skills: "He dribbles, fakes, then takes the rock to the glass." (p.10). This concise line is an excellent example of the impact of these writing strategies: it uses strong verbs such "dribbles" and "fakes" and specific nouns like "rock" and "glass" to clearly and directly convey information about Josh playing basketball. Without these specific nouns and strong verbs, the piece would be wordier, less clear, and lack some of the tone and personality of the original text: an altered version that doesn't employ these strategies might read, "He makes one basketball move, then makes another, then takes the ball toward the hoop . . . " This new sentence is longer than the original text and doesn't contain the same clarity and expression.

Step 3: Engage Students in Investigative Work
Once students understand the attributes and importance of specific nouns and strong verbs, they'll be positioned to apply their knowledge of this concept to culturally relevant communication. The guideline sheet depicted in Figure 1.1 illustrates the suggestions I give students to help them connect their understanding of this strategy to communication they encounter in their out-of-school lives. (This figure is also available in reproducible form in Appendix B.)

Before the students begin their investigations and analyses, I like to provide examples of the investigative work I ask them to do in the activity. For example, I recently discussed the impact of specific nouns to the effectiveness of an exercise class in which I participated, explaining that the names of specific pieces of exercise equipment such as "kettlebell" and "medicine ball" were essential to everyone involved in the class having clear understandings of what materials they would be using at particular times. "Without these specific nouns," I explained, "it would have been a lot harder for the instructor to clearly communicate with the participants. This is just one of the many examples of this strategy being used for effective communication outside of a school environment."

Step 4: Create Opportunities for Students to Share
This step is designed to give students the chance to share the findings of the investigative work they did in the previous component of the

Figure 1.1 Guideline Sheet for Strong Verbs and Specific Nouns in Community Conversations

Investigative Work: Strong Verbs and Specific Nouns in Community Conversations!

- In our past few classes, we've been discussing strong verbs and specific nouns. We've examined what these writing strategies are and why they're important to effective communication.
- Now, we get to put our knowledge of this strategy into action by investigating its role in the conversations we have in our communities!
- You'll do investigative work on this topic by identifying examples of strong verbs and specific you hear outside of school and reflecting on their impact.
- Use the graphic organizers below to guide your observations and analyses.

Writing Strategy Strong verb

Example

Context

Why the writing strategy is important to the effectiveness of the original statement

Writing Strategy Specific noun

Example

Context

Why the writing strategy is important to the effectiveness of the original statement

instructional process; this opportunity to share allows for students to integrate their home lives into the ELA classroom in academically relevant ways. I recently listened to fifth-grade students who had completed this activity share what specific nouns and strong verbs they noticed in community conversations; one explained that she heard many examples of these concepts in a discussion about cooking: "I was helping my sister make ox tail soup—my family has that a lot," she explained, "and I noticed that she said a ton of these [strong verbs and specific nouns]. She said a lot of strong verbs like "dice" and "sauté" to explain exactly how to cook something, and a lot of specific nouns—the names of specific ingredients—to show exactly what goes in the soup."

Step 5: Ask Students to Incorporate Strong Verbs and Specific Nouns in their Own Works and Reflect on their Impact
I recommend concluding this instructional process by asking students to apply this writing strategy to their own works and considering its importance. When I ask students to do this, I tell them that they can apply the writing tools of specific nouns and strong verbs to any genre of writing: "As you've seen in our discussions and activities," I recently told a fifth-grade class, "these writing strategies are used in—and are important to—all kinds of writing and communication. I'd like you to focus on using a specific noun and a strong verb in a piece of writing that you create. It can be something you're already working on for school, it can be something you're already writing outside of school, or it can be something you create just for this purpose."

I tell the students a specific date on which I'm going to ask them to come to class ready to discuss specific nouns and strong verbs they used, the kind of piece in which they used them, and how they made an impact on the piece. On the day this class shared its insights, one student noted that she used a number of specific nouns and strong verbs in a report for her science class, and another explained that she used these concepts when writing in a nature journal that she keeps in her free time: "I used a lot of a specific nouns and strong verbs in my nature journal," she shared. "I used specific nouns like 'fawn,' 'doe,' and 'spruce' when writing about animals and trees I saw. I used strong verbs when I said the fawn "stumbled" and the doe "sprinted." The specific nouns and strong verbs I used made an impact because they let me describe what I saw as clearly as possible."

Middle School: Sensory Details in Culturally Relevant Texts
This activity gives students the tools and understandings needed to identify and analyze the impact of sensory details on texts they encounter outside of school. The Common Core Standards emphasize the importance of this strategy, as middle-school writing standards W.6.3.D, W.7.3.D., and W.8.3.D call for students to understand the impact of this strategy and implement

in their works. This writing strategy is applied across audiences, purposes, and genres to help readers form detailed understandings of situations authors describe; a middle-school student recently explained the applicability of this strategy to me by asserting, "Whether someone's writing a novel or explaining what went down in yesterday's basketball game, sensory details are going to make the writing pop." Let's look at an instructional process for helping other middle-school students understand how sensory imagery can make "writing pop" in a variety of contexts.

Step 1: Introduce the Strategy
The first step of this instructional process is giving students a strong understanding of what sensory imagery is, so that all students are aware of the features of this concept. When introducing this strategy, I explain to students that sensory details are tools writers use to help their readers understand how they would use their senses to experience events and situations in the text if they were present, such as what they'd see, smell, taste, feel, or hear. To give students concrete understandings of this writing strategy, I show them a published excerpt from a grade-level text and identify the sensory details in it. For example, I recently shared a sensory detail-laden passage from Walter Dean Myers' short story "Block Party—145th Street Style." In this excerpt, the story's narrator, a girl named Squeezie, discusses her experience attending a neighborhood event with her friend Peaches: "Some brothers with dreads started playing steel drums and that was getting us back to a good mood. The steel drums were on the money and when Big Joe showed up with a portable grill everything was everything" (p. 143). After sharing this passage with students, I identified the sensory details that struck me and the senses with which they align: the images of people with dreadlocks and Big Joe appearing with a grill appeal to our sense of sight, while the discussion of the sound of steel drums connects to our auditory senses.

Another great example of this strategy that can illustrate its impact to students is the following excerpt from Hena Khan's (2017) novel *Amina's Voice*: "I'm pretty sure that was what Adam, the judge with the sleeve tattoos, said to the tall redheaded girl on *The Voice* last Sunday night..."(p. 3). Like the preceding example from "Big Joe's Funeral," this passage from *Amina's Voice* uses sensory details to convey key details that help readers understand the situation in depth. In this example, Khan, through Amina's narration, appeals to our sense of sight by helping us visualize the sleeve tattoos on the judge and the height and red hair of the contestant. I recommend sharing this passage with students and highlighting these examples of sensory imagery. Once students look closely at the examples described in this section from "Big Joe's Funeral" and *Amina's Voice*, they'll be ready to move on to the next part of this instructional process.

Step 2: Explain its Impact
After showing students examples of sensory imagery, I work with them on understanding the impact of that language on the text by asking them to consider the question "Why did the author use these sensory details?" Middle-school students I work with often recognize sensory details as attributes of effective writing, but many have not reflected on why this writing strategy is important. I explain to students that the use of sensory details gives the audience a clear understanding of characters' experiences and allows writers to focus on important aspects of situations (Ruday, 2016). For example, without sensory details, the previously described passage from "Block Party—145th Street Style" wouldn't allow us to understand the block party in the same level of detail as we currently do. If the language that appeals to our senses was removed, we might be left with a passage like, "The block party became more active and we were in a better mood." Without the sensory details, we wouldn't be able to imagine the sounds of the steel drums and envision sights such as the drummers' dreadlocks and the portable grill. Similarly, the excerpt from *Amina's Voice* wouldn't have the same impact on the reader without sensory language: the sensory details in the passage allow us to envision the judge's tattoos and the height and hair color of the contestant. Without them, the passage might refer to "Adam, the judge" and "the girl" instead of "Adam, the judge with the sleeve tattoos" and "the tall redheaded girl." These details allow us to picture the individuals being described more clearly, helping us understand the situation in more detail and ensuring that the reader and writer share common understandings of what's taking place.

When discussing the impact of sensory language with students, I like to emphasize that authors use this concept purposefully to focus on details that are important to the story. I've found this to be an important point to emphasize because it helps students comprehend that authors don't make decisions at random about what sensory details to incorporate; instead, they consider which details are most essential to the reader's understandings and develop those details using sensory language. This, I explain to students, is why writing that contains sensory language doesn't usually contain language that appeals to *every* sense: the author is using this strategy with a specific goal in mind, not just for the sake of using it. Authors, like Walter Dean Myers in the passage from "Block Party—145th Street Style" and Hena Khan's in *Amina's Voice* select certain details that are important to the reader's understanding of the work and use sensory language to help those details come alive for their readers.

Step 3: Ask Students to Identify and Analyze Culturally Relevant Examples
At this point in the instructional process, I give increased ownership and responsibility to the students by asking them to identify and analyze culturally relevant examples of sensory language that they encounter

outside of school. This "investigative work," as I call it when talking with students, calls for them to find and reflect on authentic, real-world examples of how the writing strategy of using sensory details is used. To guide students through this activity, I give them the guideline sheet and template depicted in Figure 1.2 and available in Appendix B.

Figure 1.2 Guideline Sheet for Identifying and Analyzing Culturally Relevant Examples of Sensory Language

---

Investigative Work: Identifying and Analyzing Sensory Language

- Recently, we've been discussing the writing strategy of sensory language; we've explored the features of this concept, examined examples of it in literature, and discussed how the use of sensory details gives the audience a clear understanding of characters' experiences and allows writers to focus on important aspects of situations.
- Today, we're taking our work with this strategy to a new level: instead of looking for examples of sensory language in literature, you're going to be identifying and analyzing how this strategy is used in real-world situations that you encounter outside of school. For example, you might notice sensory language in a song you hear, a conversation you have, a social media post or text you read, or a television show you watch.
- The graphic organizer below will help you identify and analyze examples of sensory language you encounter. It calls for you to document three examples; they can all be from the same text or different texts. The examples can relate to different senses, the same senses, or some combination (such as two examples related to the sense of sight and one to the sense of smell).

Sensory Language

Context

Related Sense

How do you think the sensory language impacts the effectiveness of the text in which it is used?

> **Sensory Language**
>
> **Context**
>
> **Related Sense**
>
> How do you think the sensory language impacts the effectiveness of the text in which it is used?
>
> **Sensory Language**
>
> **Context**
>
> **Related Sense**
>
> How do you think the sensory language impacts the effectiveness of the text in which it is used?

Step 4: Give Students the Chance to Share their Insights

Next, I recommend scheduling time for students to share the out-of-school sensory language they've identified and analyzed. I ask students to share by identifying one example of sensory language they noted on their guideline sheets, stating its context, and discussing how the sensory detail impacted the effectiveness of the text in which it was used. For example, an eighth grader recently noted, "I heard a ton of sensory language when I was watching a football game [on television] and listening to the broadcasters. One example was when the announcers were talking about how the wind was swirling around the stadium and creating really cold and difficult conditions for the players to play the game. This connected to my sense of touch because it was like I could feel the wind myself through their description of it. This language definitely made the broadcast better because it helped me really imagine what I'd feel and experience if I was there at the game."

Another student recounted a conversation with her grandmother that featured sensory language related to the sense of smell: "My grandma was telling me about a festival in our town and she was talking about how you could go anywhere at the festival and smell the pork barbecue and hush puppies that were being made, so there was a lot of sensory language about what she could smell. It was cool that she used this sensory language because it gave me a good understanding of what it was like there. If she didn't use it, I couldn't get such a good understanding of what the festival was like."

Step 5: Ask Students to Apply the Strategy of Sensory Language their Own Works and Reflect on its Impact

Now that students have demonstrated their awareness of sensory language, I suggest asking them to apply this knowledge by incorporating this writing tactic into their own works and reflecting on its importance to the effectiveness of the text in which they used it. I recently prepared an eighth-grade class to do this by reminding them of the importance of this strategy to effective writing and asking them to take three days to apply it to a piece they're writing in any genre and for any purpose. At the end of those three days, I explained, the students were to bring in an example of their writing that used sensory language and were to be prepared to discuss its significance to the piece. One student in the class described how she used sensory language in a report on the Battle of Yorktown in the American Revolutionary War: "I used a lot of sensory language to help describe the scene, like the colors of the soldiers' uniforms, the size of the battlefield and the water near it, and the sound of the cannons." Another explained that he used sensory language when writing a post on social media about standing in line to see the *Star Wars* movie, *The Last Jedi*: "I used a lot of sensory details when I posted on Facebook about waiting in line at the movie theater to get in to see *The Last Jedi*. I wrote about seeing the people dressed like characters from the movie and hearing people humming the *Star Wars* theme music. All of these details definitely made an impact on my Facebook post because they gave a lot of details about what was going on."

High School: Language Connotation in Students' Out-of-School Lives

In this activity, high-school students identify and reflect on the connotations of language they encounter in their out-of-school lives and communities. This instructional practice provides an authentic, culturally relevant application of an important writing strategy; Common Core State Standards L.9–10.5.B and L.11–12.5.B note the significance of this concept, calling for students to analyze connotative differences (or associative meanings) in the meanings in words with similar denotations (or dictionary definitions) (Core Standards, 2010). Understanding nuanced distinctions in the connotations of words with similar denotations contributes to students' college and career-readiness, as this strategy applies to a wide range of subject areas and topics: authors in science, history, and politics are frequently required to consider both the connotations and denotations of the language they use. Comprehending the connotative and denotative meanings of language in a text is essential to understanding why the author made the linguistic choices that she or he did.

Step 1: Describe the Strategy
The first step of this instructional process is to describe for students the concepts of connotation and denotation, focusing on what each one is and the differences between the two. When I've worked with high-school students on connotation and denotation, I've found that some are comfortable with the concepts, some have some general familiarity but need more information to develop their understandings, and some need to learn the fundamental components of these topics. To ensure that all students have common understandings of these terms, I recommend conducting a mini-lesson in which you explain what connotation and denotation are, provide examples of words with similar denotations but different connotations, and discuss how those words have different connotative meanings.

In a recent mini-lesson I conducted on this topic, I began by explaining that the denotation of a word is its dictionary definition and its connotation is the feelings or emotions that are typically associated with it. Next, I shared with students some word pairs that have similar denotations, but different connotations, such "thrifty and cheap," "bold and reckless," and "leisurely and lazy." I discussed how the two words in each pairing had similar denotations, but conjured up different kinds of emotions. "Let's take 'bold' and 'reckless,'" I told the students. "Both of their meanings relate to fearlessness, but one has a much more positive connotation than the other. 'Bold' is typically used in positive descriptions, such as 'The bold explorer traveled to a new land' or 'The coach made a bold call that resulted in the team's victory.' On the other hand, 'reckless' is usually used in negative ways, such as 'The quarterback's reckless play resulted in an interception' or 'Their reckless use of money led to serious financial problems.'" Once students understand the concepts of connotation and denotation and have considered some examples of words with similar denotations but different connotations, they'll be ready to move to the next step of this process.

Step 2: Explain its Impact
This instructional stage moves students to a higher, more complex level of understanding and analysis by helping them understand the importance of connotation to effective communication. I tell my students that being aware of the impact of connotation will enhance their ability to understand information and to communicate with others. "Thinking carefully about

connotation," I recently explained, "helps us reflect on the specific message an author or speaker is trying to get across. It's an essential tool to becoming a critical consumer of information, as well as a strong communicator in your own speaking and writing."

To get students to start thinking about the significance of this concept, I show them an excerpt from literature in which the connotation of a word is important to the message the author is trying to convey. For example, the connotation of the word "strangest" plays a significant role in the following sentence from *The Great Gatsby* (Fitzgerald, 1925), in which narrator Nick Carraway describes the social and physical structure of his community: "It was a matter of chance that I should have rented a house in one of the strangest communities in North America" (p. 9). The negative connotation of "strangest" is important to this sentence because it conveys Nick's unfavorable view of East and West Egg. If the sentence used a word with a similar denotation but more positive connotation, such as "unique" or "distinct," it wouldn't express Nick's attitude as accurately.

In her 2017 novel *The Hate U Give*, author Angie Thomas also uses connotation-rich language (through protagonist Starr Carter's narration) to communicate messages and attitudes to the reader. For example, the use of the words "abandoned" and "busted" in the sentence "We're on Carnation where most of the houses are abandoned and half the streetlights are busted" (p. 21) allows Starr to accurately express her perception of the neighborhood she is describing. The negative connotation of "abandoned" and "busted" conveys to the reader that Starr doesn't feel this area is kept-up very well. If Starr instead used words with positive or neutral connotations, such as "unoccupied" in place of "abandoned" and "needing repair" in place of "busted," the tone of the passage wouldn't be as negative. Since Starr is attempting to convey that the street being described is not a desirable place to be, the connotations of the terms she uses align with her message. Showing students passages such as these from *The Great Gatsby* and *The Hate U Give*, discussing with them the connotations of key terms, and helping them reflect on why an author chose those words can help them develop strong understandings of this concept's importance.

Step 3: Ask Students to Identify and Reflect on Culturally Relevant Examples of Connotation-Rich Language

This instructional step asks students to apply their knowledge of connotation by looking for examples of connotation-rich language they encounter in their out-of-school lives and cultures. To conduct this activity, students need to reflect on what they read and hear outside of school, identify words with specific connotations, explain what those connotations are, and reflect on why the connotation of those words are important to the effectiveness of the larger context in which they appear. I give students the graphic organizer depicted in Figure 1.3 (and available in reproducible form in Appendix B) to guide their work; it gives them a place to chart their observations and analysis.

Figure 1.3 Guideline Sheet for Identifying and Reflecting on Culturally Relevant Examples of Connotation-Rich Language

---

Investigative Work: Identifying and Reflecting on Out-of-School Examples of Connotation-Rich Language

- We've been working hard lately on the concept of connotation (the feelings and emotions associated with a word) and how it is similar to and different from denotation (the dictionary definition of a word).
- We looked at how words with similar denotations can have different connotations; for example, we discussed how "leisurely" and "lazy" both have denotations related to avoiding strenuous effort, but "leisurely" has a positive connotation and "lazy" has a negative one.
- After that, we discussed the importance of connotation to effective communication; we reflected on how this concept allows authors and speakers to ensure their audiences interpret their statements in the ways they intended.
- Now, you're going to take what you've learned about the importance of connotation and apply it to language you encounter outside of school. To do this, think about language you read and hear in your out-of-school communication. You might ask yourself questions like, "What are some connotations of the words I hear in my home and community?" "How does connotation impact language I encounter in extra-curricular activities, such as sports, arts, and clubs?" and "How is the concept of connotation important to information I encounter on social media?"
- To complete this activity, you'll identify two examples of connotation-rich language and analyze them. You'll use the graphic organizer provided, which asks you to identify connotation-rich language you encounter in out-of-school situations, note the relevant denotations and connotations, and reflect on why the connotation of the language you identified is important to the effectiveness of the larger communication context (such as the conversation, song, discussion, or text message) in which it was used.

Connotation-rich language you identified

Context

Denotation

Connotation

Why the connotation of the language you identified is important to the effectiveness of the communication context in which it was used

(Continued)

Figure 1.3 (Continued)

Connotation-rich language you identified
Context
Denotation
Connotation
Why the connotation of the language you identified is important to the effectiveness of the communication context in which it was used

Step 4: Schedule Time for Students to Share their Insights

I like to follow the preceding activity by making time for students to share the connotation-rich language they identified and their analyses of its importance; doing so maximizes the academic and cultural benefits of this instructional practices by valuing students' understandings of the material and the connections they make to their out-of-school lives and interests. When students get to share their findings with the rest of the class, they're given a platform to show what they know, while also making personal connections to the material. A tenth-grade student with whom I worked recently shared her connotative analysis of the word "wise" in a conversation she had with her father about an experienced basketball coach: "I just made the girls' varsity basketball team and my dad was like, 'Coach Jones is gonna help your game. He's coached for twenty-something years and is so wise.' I picked 'wise' as my connotation-rich language. Its denotation is 'intelligent,' but I think its connotation is 'experienced.' You wouldn't say that a really intelligent kid is 'wise.' You'd use a word with a different connotation instead. I think the connotation of the word 'wise' was important to the effectiveness of my dad's statement because he was talking about how Coach Jones' experience is part of the reason he can help my game." I told this student that I was impressed by how thoughtfully she shared her insights: she did a great job of identifying this word's connotation, differentiating it from other words' similar denotations, and analyzing the importance of this word's connotation to the point of her father's statement.

Step 5: Ask Students to Incorporate Connotation-Rich Language in their Own Works and Reflect on its Impact

Concluding the instructional practice in this way gives even more ownership to students by allowing them to utilize the strategy in pieces they create. When I ask students to do this, I explain that the piece of writing can be of any genre and for any audience: "Like our 'investigative work' activity showed, this writing strategy is a tool that can be used for effective communication in all kinds of contexts. Your job," I informed them, "is to bring in a piece of writing that you've created for any scenario that contains connotation-rich language. You'll describe an example of connotation-rich language you used and how it has an impact on the effectiveness of the piece." A tenth-grade student who writes poetry in her free time explained that she used the word "yearn" in a poem she wrote because of its strong connotation: "In one of my poems, I was talking about wanting to reach my goals. I used 'yearn' when talking about wanting to reach a certain goal I have because of its strong connotation. I first wrote 'want,' but I replaced it with 'yearn' because I think that word has a connotation that's stronger than 'want' does. Using a word with a powerful connotation like 'yearn' helped my poem be as powerful as possible."

Another student in the same class explained that he used the word "cramped" in a text message that explained why he left a party: "I sent my friend a text that I left a party that I had gone to. In the text, I wrote that the place was 'cramped' and that that there were too many people for me to move around. I intentionally used 'cramped' because it has a negative connotation and I was trying to show why I left the party. If I used a word with a positive connotation, my text wouldn't have made as much sense."

Key Points about Writing Strategies and Diverse Texts

- ◆ The tools of effective writing aren't limited to the types of writing students traditionally read and create in school; instead, they are present in all kinds of language students regularly encounter in their out-of-school lives and communities.
- ◆ We teachers can use culturally relevant pedagogy when working with our students on writing strategies by giving them opportunities to find examples of important, grade-level-appropriate writing strategies in authentic situations they encounter outside of the classroom.

- This instructional practice can benefit students in three key ways:
  - It can give students additional opportunities to apply their understandings of writing strategies.
  - It can help students build confidence in their knowledge of writing strategies through the use of familiar texts.
  - It can show students that their cultural backgrounds and out-of-school lives belong in school.
- When putting this idea into action in your classroom, I recommend following a five-step instructional process. The activities and texts discussed in this chapter will help you differentiate the process based on the grade level you teach by selecting strategies and activities for use in elementary, middle, and high school.
- The instructional process I recommend is:
  - Introduce the writing strategy with a mini-lesson that describes its fundamental components.
  - Discuss the importance of the strategy to effective communication, using published examples to illustrate its impact.
  - Ask students to do "investigative work" by looking for, identifying, and analyzing relevant examples of the writing strategy they encounter in their out-of-school lives and communities.
  - Schedule time for students to share the culturally relevant examples of the writing strategies they identified and analyzed.
  - Ask students to incorporate the strategy in their own works and reflect on its impact.

2

Dialect and Student Writing

In this chapter, we'll examine an essential component of culturally relevant English language arts instruction: the importance of dialect in student writing. As we'll explore further in this chapter, the dialects and language variations our students use outside of school are important aspect of their identities and valuing those forms of language in our classrooms is a key way to create a classroom that embraces students' out-of-school lives and identities. We'll begin this chapter by thinking about what it means to create opportunities for students to incorporate dialects and language variations into their writing, noting the main components of such an instructional practice. After that, we'll consider how this instructional practice can benefit our students academically and culturally. Then, we'll look at how this instructional practice can be put into action in elementary-, middle-, and high-school English and language arts classrooms. Finally, I'll share key ideas to keep in mind when using these ideas with your students.

What Is It?

The term "dialects and language variations" refers to the many forms that the English language can take, such as formal language, informal language, and linguistic structures that vary based on one's regional, ethnic, or social background (Kolln & Funk, 2012). Some ways dialects and language variations manifest themselves are through vocabulary terms (such as slang terms and regional words), word structures (such as abbreviated forms of words), and sentence constructions (which can vary across dialects and linguistic structures). Figure 2.1 contains explanations and examples of each of these types of linguistic variations.

Figure 2.1 Examples of Linguistic Variations

Linguistic Variation	Explanation	Example
Vocabulary terms	Different vocabulary terms are used sometimes used to refer to the same items due to slang terms and regional words for those items.	A long sandwich with meats and cheeses can be called a hoagie, grinder, or sub depending on one's regional background (Katz, 2016).
Word structures	Various dialects and regionalisms call for words to be shortened or adapted in different ways.	The many plural forms of "you" is an excellent example of this: "y'all" is frequently associated with southern dialects, while "y'uns" is connected with Appalachian and Midwestern dialects (Kolln & Funk, 2012).
Sentence constructions	The organization and construction of sentences often varies across dialects and linguistic structures.	The use of the word "be" to indicate a habitual action is a feature of African American English (Wheeler & Swords, 2006). Wheeler and Swords explain that the informal statement "She be talking during class" has an equivalent meaning of "She is usually talking during class."

To help students reflect on the importance of dialect and language variations in writing and then integrate this idea into to their works, I use a five-step process that helps students reflect on the importance of dialect and language variations to written works that incorporate them and then purposefully integrate those concepts in their own writing. First, I show students examples of grade-level published texts that contain examples of dialect and language variations. After that, I discuss the importance of the dialect and language variations in the texts with the students, encouraging them to reflect on how the works would be different if they didn't contain these linguistic forms and used formal language instead. Then, I engage students in "investigative work," in which they identify informal language and/or dialect they hear in their everyday lives and consider why that language is important to the statement in which it appears. Next, I help students look for opportunities to use dialects and language variations in their own writings. Finally, I ask students to reflect on the impact of those concepts on the pieces they create. Later in this chapter, we'll examine grade-specific texts and ideas to help you integrate this concept into your instruction.

How Can It Help Students?

This instructional practice can have many positive effects on students: two especially important benefits are that it can validate their home languages and identities and can help them think carefully and metacognitively about language use. In this section, we'll reflect on each one of these potential benefits.

It Can Validate Students' Home Languages and Identities

One of my strongest-held beliefs about teaching is that we educators need to respect and validate students' home languages, an idea support by research (Wheeler & Swords, 2006), policy statements (NCTE 2003), and anecdotal evidence from my experience and conversations with other teachers. I make a point to discuss this idea with the future English teachers I work with, asserting that our students' languages and identities are closely intertwined and, therefore, if we show students that we value the language they use outside of school, we'll also send the message that we value their identities, backgrounds, and cultures. For example, if we create opportunities for students to write stories in which characters use dialects and informal language, we communicate to students that we value many forms of language in our classrooms—and, by extension—a range of identities and backgrounds. When I was recently consulting in a rural school, a student asked me if it was okay if a character in her short story used "y'all." "My main character's talking with her friends and I want her to use 'y'all' she's talking to them. It's how people I know would say this and how my character would really talk," she explained. I strongly encouraged her to use this linguistic structure; she not only enhanced her piece by doing it, but also brought an aspect of her home identity in the classroom.

It Can Help Students Think Carefully and Metacognitively about Language Use

When students reflect on the uses of dialects and language variations in effective writing and ultimately incorporate this concept into their works, they develop the ability to think carefully about why different forms of language are used in various situations. When I talk with students about this concept, I assert that all forms of language are valid and important; our choice to use a particular type of language in a situation is not determined by whether language is "right or wrong," but whether or not that form of language is most aligned with the audience's expectations in a particular situation. For example, let's think about the student that asked about a character in her short story using "y'all" to enhance the story's authenticity. This is a great example of strategic language use: the character is using this term in a conversation with her friends and the author wants the language used to seem as realistic as possible. Given the informal setting and the character's attributes, it would be strange for the audience if this character communicated very formally. Applying this idea to another genre, it would be strange if an informational essay on a scientific phenomenon used informal language, as those linguistic choices wouldn't align with the language expectations associated with that piece. As students look at language variations and think about how they might apply them to their own writings, they think about the choices that accompany language, employing metacognitive thinking skills while doing so. Doing so helps students ask "Why?" and "Why not?" when they encounter the language choices authors make and equips them to take the same thoughtful approach to their own works.

How Can It Look in Action?

In this section, we'll look in depth at an instructional process designed to help students understand the importance of dialect and language variation to effective writing, apply it to their own works, and reflect on its impact on the pieces they create. This description discusses tactics for teaching this concept to upper-elementary, middle, and high-school grades, such as mentor texts, classroom excerpts, and student-work examples aligned with these grade levels. While the specific examples and uses of dialect and language variation vary across the grades described here, the key concept of understanding and appreciating purposeful and diverse language use remains the same.

Step One: Show Students Published Examples of Dialect and Language Variations

I recommend beginning this instructional process by showing students published texts containing dialect and language variations, such as informal terms, regional sayings, and other linguistic structures. This practice validates the use of informal language in writing by providing examples of times when it is effectively used, essentially communicating to students, "These published authors use dialect and informal language in their works, so you can too." I've found that students often feel they aren't allowed to use informal language when they write in school (such as the previously mentioned student who asked if it was okay if she used "y'all" in her short story). While not all writing situations are aligned with the use of informal language—a concept explored in more depth in step two of this instructional process—an important first step toward valuing students' home languages is showing them published examples of informal language and dialects.

Elementary-School Connection: *Patina*
When recently working with a group of fourth graders on the impact of dialect and informal language, I shared an excerpt from Jason Reynolds' (2017) novel *Patina,* which students had listened to as a read-aloud earlier in the year. In this passage, Patina, the book's narrator and protagonist, uses informal, dialectical language to describe her strategy for success in the 800-meter run event in track and field and how it compares the tactics used by her competitors: "Pace. That's where eight-hundred runners blow it. They start out too fast and be rigged by the second lap. I seen a lot of girls get roasted out there, showboatin' on that first four hundred. But I knew better. I knew the second four hundred was the kicker" (p. 5).

Middle-School Connection: *Bronx Masquerade*
In a conversation with an eighth-grade class about using dialect as a tool for writing, I highlighted a selection from Nikki Grimes' (2002) novel *Bronx Masquerade,* in which a character named Tyrone uses dialect and informal language to express his feelings about school: "School ain't nothin' but a joke. My moms don't want to hear that, but if it weren't for Wesley and my other homeys, I wouldn't even be here, aiight?" (p. 7).

High-School Connection: *Hip-Hop High School*
When talking about this concept with a tenth-grade English class, I displayed an excerpt from Alan Lawrence Sitomer's (2006) novel *Hip-Hop High School,* in which Theresa, the novel's narrator and protagonist, is describing a conversation with her best friend Cee. This passage, which depicts the two characters discussing the first day of school, also utilizes dialect and informal language.
 'Anyway, me and Cee, we're tight like a kite."
 'You wanna ditch class?'
 'It's the first day of school.'
'Exactly. We ain't gonna be doing nothing anyway,' she said as she checked her lipstick in a small mirror she pulled from her purse.
 'What happened to startin' fresh?' I asked.
'Yeah, maybe you right,' she said puckering her lips."(p. 3)

Step Two: Discuss the Importance of Dialect and Language Variations in the Texts
Now that students have seen published examples of dialect and informal language, they're positioned to think about why authors chose to use these linguistic forms in their works and the impact these linguistic choices have on the text. I recently explained this instructional activity

to middle schoolers by telling them, "You've seen examples of dialect and informal language in published writing, but now I want you think about why the author made these choices. Authors always have reasons behind the choices they make. We're going to talk about what the reasons might be in this situation." This approach builds students' metacognitive awareness of authors' decisions, helping them think carefully about language use and the impact of linguistic choices on effective writing. To guide students' thinking, I return to the published examples of dialect and informal language I showed them in the last step and ask them to reflect on how the excerpts would be different if the pieces instead used formal language. I like to facilitate this analysis by asking students to change examples of dialect and informal language in the passage we're discussing to formal language and then talking with them about how the original language used impacts our experience reading the piece. In this section, we'll examine examples of this activity using the dialect-infused texts and passages I shared with elementary-, middle-, and high-school classes.

Elementary-School Connection: Analyzing the Language in *Patina*

After presenting the previously described passage from *Patina* to the fourth-grade class with which I was working, I explained to the students that our next step was to consider why author Jason Reynolds decided to have Patina express her thoughts using dialectical terms like "blow it" and "showboatin" and informal, abbreviated sentence structure. "We can see that there are examples of dialect and informal language in this book," I told the students. "Jason Reynolds didn't do this by accident—he definitely had a reason for having Patina communicate this way. We're going to think together about why the author decided to have Patina use the language she does and how it impacts the story."

To get the conversation started, I displayed the original text to the front of the room: "Pace. That's where eight-hundred runners blow it. They start out too fast and be rigged by the second lap. I seen a lot of girls get roasted out there, showboatin' on that first four hundred. But I knew better. I knew the second four hundred was the kicker" (p. 5). "Now," I told the students, "let's think about what this passage would look like in formal language. This will help us really get a sense of the impact of the informal language and dialect that Jason Reynolds has Patina use."

"Let's get started with the opening section that reads 'Pace. That's where eight-hundred runners blow it.'" I continued. "Who can tell us what this might look like if it was rewritten in formal language?"

I called on a student who explained, "I think it would be more formal if it said, 'Many runners in the eight-hundred meters make mistakes with their pace.'"

"Really nice job," I replied. "I love how carefully you thought about more formal versions of the language Patina uses." I wrote the new text on the whiteboard near the projected original text. I continued to call on other students in the class who provided explanations of how sections from the passage would look if rewritten in formal language. Once the class completed its work, the new, formal version read: "Many runners in the eight-hundred meters make mistakes with their pace. They start out too fast and are tired by the second lap. I've seen a lot of girls become exhausted by going too fast on the first four hundred. However, I had a better strategy. I knew the second four was more important."

"Awesome work, all of you, on creating this formal adaptation of this excerpt from *Patina*!" I praised the students. "Now that we've looked at the original version, which contains dialect and informal language, and this revised version, which we created to use more formal language, let's think carefully about the original text: why do you think Jason Reynolds chose to have Patina communicate using dialect and informal language in the original version? Why not have her use formal language instead?"

First, I called on a student who explained, "If he had Patina use formal language, it wouldn't sound like a kid was talking."

Another student added to this comment, "Yeah, it would be really unrealistic if she spoke really formally. That's not how most people Patina's age would actually talk about running a race. They'd use more informal words and phrases, like Patina does."

"And," interjected another student in the class, "the dialect and informal language that Patina uses show her personality. If the author just had Patina use formal language, we wouldn't see her personality."

Middle-School Connection: Analyzing the Language in *Bronx Masquerade*

My eighth graders loved the dialect-rich excerpt from *Bronx Masquerade* that I showed them, so I couldn't wait to analyze the importance of that dialect to the effectiveness of the passage with them. "I know you all really liked the passage from *Bronx Masquerade* we talked about on Tuesday," I began our discussion, "and many of you commented on how much you were impressed by the use of dialect in it. Today, we're going to talk further about the dialect in this piece: we're going to discuss why Nikki Grimes, the author of this book, has Tyrone, the character speaking in that passage, use dialect, as well as why the dialect is important to our experience reading the passage."

"This is the example I showed you recently," I told the students, projecting the excerpt from *Bronx Masquerade* that we recently discussed to the front of the room: "School ain't nothin' but a joke. My moms don't want to hear that, but if it weren't for Wesley and my other homeys, I wouldn't even be here, aiight?" (p.7).

"To help us understand the importance of dialect to this passage, we're going to work together to rewrite it in more formal language that doesn't contain any of the dialect that the original text has," I explained to the students. "This will allow us to compare the two versions."

The students and I looked at the original passage and translated it sentence-by-sentence to formal language; for each sentence, I asked for volunteers to share how they think it would look if written formally. Once we completed the activity, the new version read: "I feel school is pointless. My mother would disagree with this statement, but I'm only in attendance at school because of Wesley and my other friends."

I wrote the new version on the whiteboard near the projection of the original text so that students could see the juxtaposition of both forms. After that, I asked the students to comment on what this shows us about the importance of dialect to the original version.

"I think the dialect is important because it's more fun to read and because it helps us understand Tyrone," responds a student. "It if was written formally, we wouldn't understand as much about him. After reading this, I feel like I know him."

Another student concurred, "I do feel like I know him, too. I think the dialect is important because it shows us his emotions and how strongly he feels about school. The formal language version would say what he thinks, but it wouldn't show his emotions in such a real-sounding way."

These students' comments, as well as many others in the class, conveyed the idea that dialect is important to this passage from *Bronx Masquerade* because of the way it allows readers to get a sense of Tyrone's unique identity.

High-School Connection: Analyzing the Language in *Hip-Hop High School*
When my students entered the classroom for this lesson, they found the excerpt from *Hip-Hop High School* that we recently discussed as an example of dialect and informal language projected to the front of the classroom:

"Anyway, me and Cee, we're tight like a kite.
'You wanna ditch class?'
'It's the first day of school.'
'Exactly. We ain't gonna be doing nothing anyway,' she said as she checked her lipstick in a small mirror she pulled from her purse.
'What happened to startin' fresh?' I asked.
'Yeah, maybe you right,' she said puckering her lips" (p. 3).

"We looked at this passage from Alan Lawrence Sitomer's book *Hip-Hop High School* recently," I reminded the students, "and we talked about how it's an example of dialect and informal language. Now, we're going to think about why the dialect and informal language used here is important to the effectiveness of the passage. In other words, we're thinking about why the author chose to have the characters speak in these ways instead of having them communicate using formal language."

Like I did with the fifth- and eighth-grade classes, I asked the students to revise the text so that it was written in formal language. They created the following passage:

"Cee and I are really close friends.

'Do you want to intentionally miss class?'

'I know. There won't be any rigorous instructional activities,' she said as she checked her lipstick in a small mirror she pulled from her purse.

'What about starting the new year off well' I asked.

'Yes, perhaps you're correct,' she said puckering her lips."

Once the students completed the revised version, I read both forms out loud. When I read the new, formal text, several students chuckled. "I noticed that some of you laughed at the version that we revised and made more formal. What do you notice when you compare the two passages?"

"They're so different!" exclaimed one student. "Even though they basically say the same things, the two passages have totally different feels to them."

"That's a great insight," I respond. "You're absolutely right that there is a different feel to the original passage compared to the revised version that we made. That comment you made is a great way for us to transition to the focus question of the day: why is the dialect and informal language in the original passage important to its effectiveness?"

"The characters would seem completely different without the dialect," replied a student. "They wouldn't seem like high-school students—they'd seem like old ladies playing bridge or something."

"It also wouldn't feel like teenagers talking to their friends if the characters used," added another student. She continued to explain, "Teenagers can use formal language sometimes, but usually they use language like this with their friends."

After a few other students provided similar comments, I provided closure to the day's discussion: "I'm thrilled by your insightful points about the significance of the dialect and informal language to this passage from *Hip-Hop High School*. You did a great job of reflecting on the way the dialect in this passage helps create relatable and realistic characters that communicate in ways that are aligned with the situation. Really nice job!"

Step Three: Engage Students in Investigative Work

After students have thought carefully about the impact of dialect and informal language on published texts, I ask them to apply their knowledge of this topic to their own lives. To do this, I ask students to conduct "investigative work," in which they identify informal language and/or dialect they encounter in their lives and reflect on the importance of that language to the effectiveness of the statement in which it was used. To facilitate this analysis, I give students a graphic organizer on which to record their observations. This template, depicted in Figure 2.2 and available in Appendix B, asks students to identify examples of dialect and/or

Figure 2.2 Graphic Organizer for Student Identification and Analysis of Dialect and/or Informal Language

---

Investigative Work: Identifying and Analyzing Dialect and Informal Language

- We've been thinking lately about the importance of dialect and informal language: we looked at a published text that contains these language features and discussed why the author may have chosen to use dialect and informal language in that work.
- In this activity, you're going to apply our knowledge of this topic to the language you encounter in your out-of-school life.
- First, you'll identify an example of dialect or informal language you hear or read in your everyday life. (Some possible situations in which you might notice these language forms are conversations in which you participate, dialogue that takes place around you, interactions in films or television shows, songs you hear, text messages you receive, and communication you find on social media. There are many other possibilities as well!) Then, you'll note the context in which that language was used. Finally, you'll then reflect on why the language used was important to the effectiveness of the communication—in other words, why the speaker or author chose to use dialect and inform
- You'll do this identification and analysis twice using the graphic organizer below and the one on the next page.

Example of dialect or informal language

Context in which it was used

Why the language used was important to the effectiveness of the communication

Example of dialect or informal language
Context in which it was used
Why the language used was important to the effectiveness of the communication

informal language they hear or read, state the context in which it appeared, and reflect on why the kind of language used was important to the effectiveness of the communication.

I use the same graphic organizer for the elementary-, and middle-, and high-school students I teach, since I ask students of each grade to do the same fundamental analysis. The difference between the grade levels emerges from the different examples the students identify and the specifics of the students' analyses. Before students begin working on this activity, I like to model my own analysis by sharing examples of informal and dialectical language I've encountered and my thoughts on the importance of the language used. I like to vary these models based on the grade level I'm teaching so that I can be sure to present my students with accessible and grade-appropriate examples. For example, I recently shared with my fifth graders an example of informal language I heard while watching basketball, while I talked with a group of high-school students about dialect featured in a popular hip-hop song. Both instances facilitated grade-level conversations about the use of these linguistics in their contexts and the importance of their use to the effectiveness of the pieces in which they were used, while also giving students models of what the activity can look like. Now, let's look inside elementary-, middle-, and high-school classrooms and consider how students I worked with completed this activity.

Elementary-School Connection

On a recent Friday afternoon in fifth grade, the students with whom I was working were excited about the academic content of the day: we were about to share the results of our investigative work on dialect and informal language. I began by calling the class together: "Today, we'll be sharing what we found in our investigative projects, where we looked for examples of dialect and informal language in our everyday lives, identified the context in which the language was used, and reflected on why the language used was important to the effectiveness of the communication. You did this twice on the graphic organizer I gave you; I'm going to ask you to share one of those examples with the rest of the class so that we can all learn from your observations and insights. Who would like to go first?"

I first called on a student who identified informal language in a conversation between her older brothers: "My two brothers were talking about a test they took in school. One of them said he aced the test and the other was talking about how he bombed it. 'Aced' and 'bombed' are both informal language. The informal language was important because it went along with the casual conversation they were having. If they used formal language, it would have sounded weird." This student's comment that formal language "would have sounded weird" in the context her brothers were having showed great insight into the importance of purposeful language variation; it conveyed her understanding that individuals adapt the linguistic forms they use for the audiences with whom they communicate and the nature of the communication. She continued to explain, "If my brothers were talking to my parents about their grades, they probably would have been more formal."

Middle-School Connection

When I recently spoke with a group of middle schoolers about their work on this activity, a student identified the word "baller" as an example of dialectical and informal language that he heard. "I was listening to the radio," he explained, "and the DJ described Jay-Z as an 'all-around baller' because of all the ways he's successful, like having a lot of popular rap songs over time and being a businessman and sports agent."

"The word 'baller' is definitely informal language," continued the student, "and the way the DJ used it was effective. It was effective because using 'baller' is a lot more interesting and sounds a lot more exciting than saying something more formal like 'successful musician and businessman' or 'powerful individual.' These words wouldn't have been as interesting to the audience and wouldn't have kept the listeners listening to the station like 'baller' probably did." This analysis shows the student's understanding of informal and formal ways to express a similar idea. In addition, it illustrates this student's awareness that a radio host would want to engage the audience and use language that does so.

High-School Connection

A high-school student who shared her work on this assignment with her classmates and me noted all of the ways she hears peers shorten words in their informal communication, saying "adorbs" for "adorable" and "fab" for "fabulous."

"People I talk with [shorten their words] all the time. I'm sure it sounds silly to some people, but I think it's actually really smart. We only say these things to each other, and even then it's on social media or text when you don't usually want to spend a lot of time or space writing. We don't use them in job interviews or on school essays—it's language we use with each other for a purpose." This student's insights are particularly noteworthy because she not only identifies the audience for these examples of informal language, but also the medium on which they are most often used. As she suggests, these choices are purposeful, done with specific benefits in mind, and are used in carefully selected situations. These informal, abbreviated words are important to effective communication because they establish a casual tone and eliminate extra space when used in digital communication.

Step Four: Help Students Purposefully Use Dialects and Language Variations in their Own Writings

At this stage in the instructional process, I ask students to consider ways to use dialect and informal language in their own works. When I talk with students about utilizing these language forms, I stress that doing so must be done purposefully. "The authors we've examined that have used dialect and informal language in their writings did this very carefully and intentionally," I recently explained to a group of eighth graders. "They thought about what forms of language would best communicate certain information to the reader and then chose to use that language in their writing. For example, remember the excerpt from *Bronx Masquerade* that we analyzed? We talked about the piece would be really different if Tyrone used formal language; he wouldn't seem as real and authentic when he expressed his thoughts about school if he communicated formally."

With students of all grade levels, I emphasize that it's important to think about the kind of language a character would use in a situation and why she or he would use that language. "Don't use informal language just for the sake of doing it," I recently reminded a group of students. "Think about the character and the setting and whether or not that language would align with who the character is and the context in which he or she is communicating." The main goal of using dialect and informal language, I explain, is to make the communication in a piece of writing as authentic as possible. In real life, all people don't use the same language all the time; the best writing also demonstrates this same language variety.

It's also important to emphasize to students to not use stereotypical language or to make generalizations when they write. I recently explained to a class of tenth graders that the language a character uses should align with her or him as an individual and not be based on the person's background or any other general attributes. "The authors we read that used informal language made sure that the informal language they used was based on that particular character, not on any sort of stereotype," I told the students. "Make sure you keep that same careful awareness in mind when you write."

Now, let's take a look at some ways students I've worked with have applied this strategy to their works.

Elementary-School Connection

I recently conferred with an elementary-school student who did a great job of using dialects and language variations to distinguish between the characters in a story he was writing. In this student's story, a ten-year-old boy and his grandfather take a trip together and grow closer as a result. The following excerpt from this student's work illustrates the distinctions in how these characters communicate and the connection between this language variation and the characters' traits.

Middle-School Connection

A middle-school student with whom I recently worked used dialect and informal language when crafting a piece about a football player. This player, who plays the position of wide-receiver, uses linguistic choices such as "I'm a burner" and "…cuz we'll have a TD in no time at all" to express his enthusiasm for the game and his confidence in his abilities. Figure 2.4 contains an excerpt from this student's writing; this passage,

Figure 2.3 Example of Elementary-School Student Writing Featuring Dialect and Language Variations

> When we finally reached my house, I told my grandfather how great the trip was. "Gramps, you're the best. This trip has been off the hook. For real."
> "Well, Connor, I'm not sure I understand all of those words, but it sounds like they are positive," he replied, smiling. "I think you're the best, also."
> "We gotta do this again soon," I said before opening the door. "It was a blast."

Figure 2.4 Example of Middle-School Student Writing Featuring Dialect and Language Variations

> The first thing you should know about me is that I'm a burner. My speed should be illegal. If the QB gets me the ball in the open field, I'm gone. Straight to the house. Put six points up on the scoreboard, cuz we'll have a TD in no time at all. Bye bye, defenders.

Figure 2.5 Example of High-School Student Writing Featuring Dialect and Language Variations

> "You got us lost again! Seriously? Come on!"
> "I'm sorry. I didn't mean to."
> "This the second time this month. I can't even. Why won't you just use the GPS for directions?"
> "I wanted to use the map."
> "Okay, but you need to at least check the map with the GPS directions. I can't do this anymore. We need to break up."
> We live in a world with many technological innovations. Cell phones are powerful computers that we can hold in our hands. Programs like Facetime allow us to see our friends and family when we want to communicate with them. Satellite radio makes it so that we don't need to find new radio stations when we drive from one city to the next. GPS programs on our phones and in our cars dramatically reduce the likelihood of getting lost. (The conversation above shows what might happen if you get lost too many times and frustrate your significant other!) Technology has the ability to improve our lives in a variety of ways if we embrace those possibilities.

which opens the story, uses linguistic choices to convey the narrator's personality and his passion for football.

In addition to the informal language used in this piece, the author also uses some informal sentence structure—in the form of short, direct statements—to express the narrator's statements about his football skill such as "Straight to the house." As we'll explore further later on in this chapter, these fragments help express the narrator's confidence and enhance the characterization in the piece.

High-School Connection
I recently spoke with a high-school student who purposely used informal language in the introduction to an argument essay he was writing about the positive impact of technology on today's society. In the excerpt depicted in Figure 2.5, the author uses informal language to create a fictional, yet realistic, conversation between two people who have just gotten lost because they didn't use their GPS to find the best way to reach their destination. This conversation is meant to introduce the idea that technology makes people's daily lives easier and reduces stress in a variety of ways. In it, characters use informal language such as "Come on!" and "I can't even" to express emotions.

Step Five: Ask Students to Reflect on How the Dialect and Language Variations They Used in their Writings Enhanced their Works

In this final instructional step, students apply the critical thinking skills they've been developing throughout this instructional process to their uses of dialect and informal language to their own writing. When I ask my students to do this, I begin by pointing out that they've already done this same kind of work when analyzing published texts and examples from their out-of-school lives; now they get to apply these reflective abilities to their own writings. "You've done this with other works," I recently told a group of middle schoolers. "Your writing deserves the same careful analysis and attention, so your job now is to think about how the dialect and informal language you used in your writing enhanced its effectiveness." To facilitate their analyses, I ask the students two related reflection questions: 1) How did the dialect and informal language you used help your piece of writing? 2) How would your piece be different if you hadn't used dialect and informal language? These questions require students to think about the impact of these linguistic forms on the pieces they create and analyze that language just as they did with other texts earlier in the instructional process. Now, let's take a look at how the student authors of the previously mentioned excerpts analyzed the importance of language variations to their pieces.

Elementary-School Connection
The elementary-school student who used informal and dialectical terms like "off the hook" and "for real" in the dialogue of his story about a ten-year-old boy who takes a trip with his grandfather explained that the language he used in the story was important for helping readers differentiate between characters in his piece and make inferences about them. "The different kinds of language that Connor [the story's protagonist] and his grandpa use are important to the story. If they both spoke the same way, you couldn't tell which character was talking without me saying which one was talking. Also, since they speak differently, you can tell more about their personality, like how Connor's pretty casual and informal and his grandpa isn't. If they spoke the same way, you couldn't tell all of this." These observations convey the author's understandings of the importance of dialect and language variation to the effectiveness of his piece.

Middle-School Connection
The middle-school student who created the dialect and informal-language infused piece told from the perspective of a confident football player asserted that the language choices he made when writing this piece were essential to expressing the protagonist's unique personality: "If I didn't make my character talk the way he does, the reader wouldn't understand how cocky he is and how much he's sure that he's the best. If he said things like 'I'm good at football and possess a great deal of speed,' the reader would still know some really basic stuff, but that's all. No one would be able to understand his personality and attitude if talked this way. The way he talks is really important for understanding this." What I especially love about this student's reflection is his awareness of the relationship between the

character's language and the way the reader is able to grasp that character's identity. For example, the student expresses that the basic information in the passage would be the same if the character expressed this information about his abilities in much more formal way, but we as readers wouldn't be able to really know the character as a person the way we do.

High-School Connection
The high-school student who created the argument essay about technology's ability to improve our lives used informal language to accurately and realistically convey an individual's frustration about getting lost. This student asserted that the "dialect and informal language helped the essay because I used it to create a beginning scene that was fun to read and relatable. People can relate to the character in the scene because she uses language that real people might use when they're frustrated." When responding to the second response question about how the piece would be different if he hadn't used dialect and informal language, the student noted that "this scene wouldn't seem as realistic. The language that the frustrated character uses show her emotion and how she's feeling. If I just used really formal language, the scene wouldn't show that."

Key Points about Dialect and Student Writing

- The term "dialects and language variations" refers to the many forms that the English language can take, such as formal language, informal language, and linguistic structures that vary based on one's regional, ethnic, or social background (Kolln & Funk, 2012).
    - Some ways dialects and language variations manifest themselves are through vocabulary terms (such as slang terms and regional words), word structures (such as abbreviated forms of words), and sentence constructions (which can vary across dialects and linguistic structures).
- By discussing the importance of dialects and language variations to effective writing with our students, we can validate students' home languages and identities and can help them think carefully and metacognitively about language use.
    - This practice can validate students' home languages and identities because students' languages and identities are closely intertwined. If we show students that we value the language they use outside of school, we'll also send the message that we value their identities, backgrounds, and cultures.
    - It can help students think carefully and metacognitively about language by developing their abilities to think carefully about why different forms of language are used in various situations.

- When putting this idea into action in your classroom, I recommend following a five-step instructional process. The activities and texts discussed in this chapter will help you differentiate the process based on the grade level you teach by selecting strategies and activities for use in elementary, middle, and high school.
- The instructional process I recommend is:
  - Show students published examples of dialect and language variations.
  - Discuss the importance of dialect and language variations in the texts.
  - Engage students in investigative work, in which they look for and analyze examples of dialects and language variations in their out-of-school lives.
  - Help students purposefully use dialects and language variations in their own writings.
  - Ask students to reflect on how the dialect and language variations they used in their writings enhanced their works.

Section 2

Culturally Relevant Reading Instruction

3

Applying Reading Strategies to Texts that Represent Diverse Backgrounds

In this chapter, we'll examine another important component of culturally relevant English and language arts instruction: the practice of applying reading strategies to texts that represent diverse backgrounds. We'll begin with an overview discussion of what it means for teachers to do this; after that, we'll reflect on why applying reading strategies to texts that represent diverse backgrounds is so important to our students' experiences in school. Next, we'll explore how this practice can look in action by considering an instructional process I've used with elementary-, middle-, and high-school students. Finally, I'll present key points to keep in mind when putting the ideas discussed in this chapter into action in your classes. (In this chapter, I'll describe examples of texts I've used with my students that represent diverse backgrounds; Appendix C of this book, "Classroom Library Recommendations: Multicultural Texts by Grade Level" provides some additional titles to consider using with your students.)

What Is It?

In this instructional practice, teachers and students apply strategies essential to effective reading—such as making connections, creating inferences, analyzing word choice, asking questions, summarizing, and forming predictions—to texts that represent a wide range of backgrounds, cultures, and experiences. When I use this instructional process in my classrooms, I begin by introducing a reading strategy that the students are ready to learn through mini-lessons on what the strategy is and why it's important to effective reading. Next, I model my use of the strategy by applying it to a range of texts that encompass diverse characters, identities, and perspectives. After that, I ask students to apply the strategy on which we're focusing to texts of their choice. Finally, I help students reflect on how the strategy they used helped them make sense of the texts they read. This instructional practice emphasizes the use of culturally diverse literature in the elementary, middle, and high-school classroom and uses those texts to help students learn about and apply important reading strategies. In the next section, we'll examine in depth why doing this can benefit our students.

How Can It Help Students?

The application of reading strategies to texts that represent diverse backgrounds, experiences, and identities helps build a culturally relevant and inclusive classroom environment. By bringing a range of cultures and voices into the classroom in ways that help students learn key reading strategies, we can help students see themselves reflected in the curriculum—which Bishop (1990) refers to as "mirrors"—and give students opportunities to learn about others' cultures and experiences—which Bishop (1990) calls "windows." In this section, we'll look closely at each of these benefits, reflecting on what each one can mean for our students.

It Can Help Students See Themselves Reflected in the Curriculum

Many of the texts students encounter in schools are limited in perspective, with the majority of books students are taught consisting "mainly of White, middle class representations" (Tschida, Ryan, & Ticknor, 2014, p. 28). Providing students with texts that represent a wide range of cultures, backgrounds, and identities can address this problem, allowing more students to see themselves reflected in the curriculum through the inclusion of narratives that describe individuals with similar experiences. When all students see their identities and backgrounds represented in texts they encounter in schools, the result is an inclusive, culturally sensitive environment that maximizes student motivation (Kumar, Zusho, & Bondie, 2018).

My experiences in the classroom and my conversations with students and teachers support these ideas and findings. I recently worked spoke with an eighth-grade English teacher who commented on the positive impact that using a diverse array of texts in her read-alouds and mini-lessons had on her classroom environment. She explained, "This year, I focused a lot on using diverse books for my read-aloud period at the beginning of class and when I modeled a reading strategy during a mini-lesson. I went to the library and looked for books that showed a lot of different cultures. I really think this helped motivate all my students because I had a diverse class and the books I used represented so many different cultures. All the students were able to see characters they could relate to." A student in this teacher's class echoed her sentiments: "I like how the books [the teacher] used in class had characters from different races. A lot of books we see in school have mostly White characters, even though our class has people from all different races. I think all these different types of characters with different background helped people feel included." These comments convey the positive impact that can result from students seeing themselves represented in the texts they encounter in school.

It Can Give Students Opportunities to Learn About Others' Cultures and Experiences

Including a diverse range of texts that represent a number of backgrounds and cultures doesn't just benefit the students who are directly represented in those books: it can enhance the learning experiences of all students by helping learn about other cultures and experiences. Reading multicultural texts gives students opportunities they might not otherwise have to learn about different backgrounds and identities; Tschida, Ryan, and Ticknor (2014) support this idea by asserting that "books are sometimes the only place where readers may meet people who are not like themselves, who offer alternative worldviews" (p. 28). By encountering these different viewpoints, students can deepen their understandings of the world around them, allowing them to achieve more developed understandings of society. As children's-book author Ebony Elizabeth Thomas explains, "It's all kids who need all stories about all kinds of people" (Thomas, 2018, n.p.).

I recently spoke with a fifth-grader who had a powerful experience reading the novel *A Long Pitch Home* by Natalie Dias Lorenzi (2016), which describes the experiences of a ten-year-old Pakistani boy named Balal who must suddenly move to the United States. The student explained that the book taught him "a lot about Pakistani culture, like how popular playing cricket is, what the foods they eat are, and other things about what life is like there." He continued to explain, "I also learned a lot about what it's like to adapt to American culture for someone who moved from somewhere else. I never had to do that since I've never moved to a new country, so I learned a lot about what that's like." This student's comments embody the benefits of reading about different background and identities that researchers and theorists identify: by reading this book, he learned about new cultures and developed understandings of others' experiences that differ from the events of his life. All of our students can learn and grow and in similar ways by reading diverse texts that help them understand other cultures and backgrounds.

How Can It Look in Action?

In this section, we'll look closely at an instructional process that uses diverse texts to teach students to think metacognitively about reading strategies. This process contains five steps: 1) Introduce a reading strategy to students, 2) Explain why the concept is important to effective reading, 3) Model the strategy by applying it to a diverse range of texts, 4) Help students apply the focal concept to a text of their choice, and 5) Ask students to reflect on how the strategy helped them make sense of the text they read. This process teaches students to use and understand reading strategies, exposes them to texts that represent diverse backgrounds, and incorporates student choice—all while building metacognition.

In the description of each step, I discuss how I taught specific reading strategies to fifth, eighth, and tenth grade classes, identifying excerpts from diverse literature I used with each of these grade levels. I selected the strategies described in these examples based on the school's curriculum map and state standards; however, you can use this process to teach any applicable and grade-appropriate reading strategy to your students. In addition, while the texts discussed in these activities are ones I've used with success, you're welcome to incorporate other multicultural texts if you would prefer—and you may want to consult the list of diverse texts in Appendix C to help guide your selection. Now, let's examine this instructional process and possible texts you can use when putting it into action!

Step One: Introduce a Reading Strategy to Students
The first step is to introduce to students the specific reading strategy that you're going to be asking them to use and reflect on as this instructional process develops. When I introduce a strategy, I conduct a mini-lesson on the key components of the strategy. This discussion prepares the students for the rest of instructional process, providing the foundation they need as they consider why the strategies are important and apply them to their own reading experiences. In this section, we'll look at how I introduced the strategies of making connections, forming inferences, and analyzing the impact of an author's word choice on a piece's mood to elementary-, middle-, and high-school students, respectively.

Elementary-School Connection
A class of eager fifth graders settled into their spots on the classroom's carpet for a reading mini-lesson. I stood in front of them next to an easel pad containing a piece of chart paper, on which I had written the words "Making Connections." "Today," I began, "we're going to talk about something that good readers frequently do when they read—they make connections to other things that the events, characters, and topics in the book make them think of." Under the phrase "Making Connections" written on the chart paper, I write the words "Events, Characters, Topics." I continued to explain, "There are three main types of connections readers make: text-to-self (which is when the book reminds you of something in your own life), text-to-text (which is when the book makes you think of another book, or another kind of text, such as a poem, song, movie, or

television show), and text-to-world (which is when the book makes you think about a real-world issue—either a current or a historical one)." On the chart paper, I drew three circles, word-web style, extending from the information I'd already written on the paper. In one circle, I wrote "text-to-self," in another, I wrote "text-to-text," and in the third circle, I wrote "text-to-world." "In our coming classes," I told the students, "we're going to talk more about this reading strategy of making connections—we'll think about why it's important, what it looks like, and how and why you can apply it to your own reading experiences."

Middle-School Connection

My eighth graders recently returned from lunch to find the words "Making Inferences" written on a piece of chart paper in front of the classroom. "Today," I said, introducing them to the lesson, "we're going to talk about one of the most important actions readers take when comprehending a text: making inferences." I continued, explaining the concept: "Authors don't normally come out and tell us everything about the characters in their books in really direct language. For example, they don't normally say 'This character is kind' or 'This character is selfish.' Instead, they describe characters' actions, statements, interests, and thoughts and leave us as readers to make inferences about the characters based on the information provided. It's what people sometimes call 'reading between the lines.'" I wrote "Reading between the lines" on the chart paper underneath "Making Inferences." Around this text, I wrote possible information readers can use to make these inferences: actions, statements, interests, thoughts." I then communicated to the students that this concept will figure prominently in our coursework: "We're going to be talking a lot in the near future about making inferences while reading: in our next class, we'll discuss why they're important to effective readers. Then, I'll model some examples of the strategy. After that, I'll ask you to use it on your own and reflect on its importance."

High-School Connection

On a recent Monday morning, I began a mini-lesson with a class of tenth graders by writing "Mood" on a piece of chart paper. "The word 'mood' is often associated with our feelings, like what kind of mood we're in and if an event in our lives puts us in a good or bad mood." Several students nodded and I continued: "However, identifying the mood an author creates is also a reading strategy. In any piece of writing, an author will choose specific words to create a certain kind of mood." Under the word "Mood" on the chart paper, I wrote "Created by author through word choice." I further explained the concept by identifying different examples of moods authors may create: "Through her or his word choice, an author might create a mood of suspense, one of excitement, or one of disappointment." To follow up on this statement, I wrote "suspense, excitement, disappointment" in separate word-web bubbles extending from the text in the middle of the chart paper. "We're going to be thinking about this reading strategy," I tell the students. "We'll talk about why considering the mood an author creates through word choice is important to strong reading and look at different examples of how word choice creates a particular mood. I'm excited to talk with you about your insights into how the authors you enjoy create moods in their work."

Step Two: Explain Why the Concept is Important to Effective Reading
Now that you've introduced a focal reading strategy to students, the next step is talk with students about why good readers use this concept and how it enhances their abilities to read effectively. When I do this with my students, I make connections to metacognition by explaining that excellent readers not only use strategies to make sense of what they read, but also identify the strategies they utilize and how those strategies help them understand the text. The concepts described in this chapter help students achieve deep understandings of the texts they read by going beyond surface-level understandings and using higher-order thinking skills to make sense of what they read. In this section, I'll discuss how I helped fifth, eighth, and tenth graders understand the importance of the respective reading strategies I introduced to them.

Elementary-School Connection
One day after I introduced to my fifth graders the concept of making connections while reading, I gathered them at the rug again for a follow-up conversation. I displayed the chart paper containing the word-web I created on the concept and explained our focus for the day: "Yesterday, we talked about the reading strategy of making connections while reading. We discussed how readers often make text-to-self, text-to-world, and text-to-text connections when they read. Can someone remind us what those connections mean?" I called on a student who shared the definitions of each of those connection types and then I continued: "Great job! Today, we're going to build off of the information we discussed yesterday by thinking about why making connections is important to effective reading."

I turned the pad of chart paper to a new page and wrote "Why is Making Connections Important to Effective Reading?" on the top. "One reason this strategy is important," I told the students, "is that it requires you to understand what's going on in the text: to make connections to the material in a book, you first need to comprehend what's taking place." I wrote "Requires reader to understand what's taking place in the book" on the chart paper. Next, I explained, "Another reason that this strategy is important is because it makes you read actively. If you're making connections to yourself, other texts, or the issues in the world while you read, you need to be actively engaged in the reading process by reflecting on what's taking place in the book and connecting that information to other knowledge you have." As I follow up to this point, I wrote, "Makes you actively engaged in the reading process." I then shared a third and final point with the class: "There's one more reason I want to share with you about why making connections is important to effective reading: doing this helps you remember what you read. Connecting the information in a book to experiences, topics, and other texts helps you recall the material in the book because you've thought carefully about it and actively engaged with it. If you had just read the material in a book but not being so active in your reading, you probably wouldn't be able to recall the events of the text as easily." To summarize this final benefit, I wrote "Helps you recall what you read" on the chart paper. I concluded this mini-lesson by previewing our upcoming work on this concept: "In our next discussion on making connections, I'll demonstrate what it can look like to make connections with reading. After you see this demonstration, we'll talk about what you noticed and how you can apply what this same skill to your own reading."

Middle-School Connection
"Yesterday, we talked about what it means to make inferences while reading," I began a reading mini-lesson with my eighth graders. Pointing to the chart paper we created in the previous day's conversation, I explained, "As we discussed, when we read, we use information like characters' actions, statements, interests, and thoughts to infer those characters' traits and attributes. Today," I continued, "we're going to talk about why this strategy is important to reading. In other words, we'll explore why it's something that good readers do." I wrote "Why Is Making Inferences Important to Effective Reading?" on a new piece of chart paper. "The first reason making inferences is important," I told the students, "is it requires readers to comprehend the information in the text. After all, we readers can't make inferences about a character unless we know what the author is saying. For example, we can't infer that a character is generous unless we understand the details in the text that show his or her generosity." I wrote "Requires readers to comprehend the information in the text" on the chart paper.

"The next reason making inferences is important" I continued, "is it helps readers develop in-depth understandings of the material in a book." I then wrote "Helps readers develop in-depth understandings" on the chart paper. "Readers who make inferences develop these in-depth understandings because they think carefully about the attributes characters possess and why they possess them. When we make inferences, we're thinking in detail about what characters are like and what evidence from the text helps us make that determination. The process of reaching these conclusions about what attributes characters possess and how we know that they possess them creates strong and detailed understandings in our minds about the text."

"There's one more reason I want to share with you about why making inferences is important to effective reading," I explained to the students. "Doing this helps us readers determine if a character changes throughout the course of a book and how she or he does so." To follow up on this statement, I wrote "Helps reader determine if a character changes" on the chart paper. I then explained the idea in more detail: "Making inferences helps us understand the characters we read about. Since character change is an important part of any book, we can develop strong understandings of the ways characters change by making inferences about them throughout a text. For example, we might look at how a character acts early in a novel and then examine how she acts later in the book after the text's major events have taken place. If the character has changed in a meaningful way, we'll probably make different inferences about her at different points in the novel."

I ended the conversation with a preview of what we'd do in our next discussion: "Next time, I'll model some examples of making inferences from published texts and talk about how my experiences making those inferences create the benefits we discussed today: comprehending the material in a book and developing in-depth understandings of the material."

High-School Connection

When my tenth graders entered the classroom for a recent meeting, they saw that I had displayed the graphic organizer we created the previous day on the reading strategy of identifying the mood an author creates. "Are we talking more about mood, today, Dr. R?" inquired a student.

"We are," I replied, "but today we're going beyond what we did yesterday. I'm sure you remember that yesterday I introduced the idea that authors will use specific words in their pieces to create a certain kind of mood, like one of suspense, excitement, or disappointment. Today," I continued to explain, "we're going to think about why thinking about the mood an author creates is important to effective reading." I wrote "Why Is Identifying Mood Important to Effective Reading?" on a new piece of chart paper.

"One reason this strategy is important," I explained, "is that it requires us readers to look carefully at the word choice and language in a piece of writing to determine the mood the author is trying to create. For example, for us to know that an author wants to create a really suspenseful mood in her novel, we'll need to look carefully and closely at the language she uses in the book to make this determination. If we just read the piece quickly without a lot of attention to the specific language choices the author makes, we won't be able to determine the mood she or he is trying to create." I wrote "Requires readers to look carefully at word choice" on the chart paper. "Another reason this strategy is important," I continued, "is thinking about the mood an author creates helps readers analyze the impact of the author's decisions." I wrote "Helps readers analyze impact of author's decisions" on the chart paper. "This benefit," I explained, "extends from the first one—after we look closely and carefully at the language in a piece, we can then analyze how that language has a particular effect. For example, if an author described clouds as 'ominous,' a building as 'haunted,' and the floors of that building as 'creaking,' we'd know that the author is trying create a spooky mood that can frighten readers. For us to make this determination, we need to identify what words the author used and think critically about the impact of that language." As I did with the other classes, I ended this discussion with a preview of our upcoming work: "In our next class meeting, I'm going to show you an example of what it looks like when a reader identifies the mood an author creates. After that, I'll turn you loose on your own and ask you to apply this strategy to your own readings."

Step Three: Model the Strategy by Applying it to a Diverse Range of Texts
This step of the instructional process has two objectives: first, to show students what the focal strategy looks like in action by modeling its use for them and second, to use diverse texts when doing so in order to include a wide range of cultures and perspectives in the classroom. When I model a reading strategy for students, I verbally call attention to what I'm doing as a reader and how doing so helps me make sense of the text, providing an example of the attributes and benefits I discussed with students in the first two steps of the process. By using diverse books for this activity, I send the message that I value a wide range of backgrounds and identities and want those perspectives to be incorporated in our academic work. I've found that doing this has helped students who are often underrepresented in the curriculum feel like their identities are valued; one eighth-grade student of color explained, "It meant a lot when that you did a lot of read-alouds with people of color in them. There were more people like me in those books than in what I saw and read about in a lot of the classes I've had before. It made me feel a lot more comfortable." Now, let's see what this instructional step can look like in action.

Elementary-School Connection
"I'm really excited for our conversation today," I begin class by telling my fifth graders. "As I'm sure you remember, we've been talking lately about making connections while reading—first, we talked about what it means to do this and then we discussed why using this strategy is important to effective reading. Now, I'm going to model what it looks like to make connections when reading and talk with you about why making connections helps me as a reader. Over the next couple of classes, I'm going to model this strategy with some different books. The first one we're going to use is *Brown Girl Dreaming* by Jacqueline Woodson (2014)."

I shared three excerpts from the text, modeling an example of a connection with each one. I made a text-to-self connection when I shared the selection "Some days we miss the way the red dirt lifted up and landed against our bare feet. Here the sidewalks burn hot all summer long" (p. 147), explaining "This passage reminds me of my own experience moving from a rural place to a city. I grew up in a rural area of Florida where I could walk barefoot outside, like Jacqueline Woodson describes doing; when I moved to New York City, like Jacqueline Woodson did, I definitely couldn't do that—there was a lot more concrete! She and I had similar reactions to adjusting to a new location." Next, I modeled an example of a text-to-world connection: "On the first page of this book, Woodson identifies and describes her birthplace by saying, 'Columbus, Ohio, USA—a country caught between Black and White' (p. 1). I can make a text-to-world connection to her description of the country. Race and equality are still widely discussed issues in the United States today. This connection helps me reflect on the topics Woodson identifies and their continued relevance." Finally, I shared an example of a text-to-text connection: "In this book, Jacqueline Woodson describes her father's football skill by saying 'Coaches were watching the way he moved, his easy stride, his long arms reaching up, snatching the ball from its soft pocket of air' (p. 15). I can make a text-to-text connection to this: I recently read an article in *Sports Illustrated* about NFL running back Saquon Barkley titled 'Face of the NFL? Saquon Barkley Has a Plan.' The author of that article, Ben Baskin, described Barkley's football abilities using similar descriptive language as Woodson did when discussing her father."

I concluded my discussion of these connections with a closing point about how making these connections enhanced my experience reading *Brown Girl Dreaming*: "Making text-to-self, text, and world connections while reading this book required me to understand the text and be active in the reading process. If I didn't understand the book, I couldn't make accurate connections to it; in addition, I wouldn't have been able to make these connections if I didn't get actively involved in thinking about what I read and how it relates to me, the world, and other things I've read. I think making these connections will help me remember what I read a lot more than if I read the text without doing this." In our next class meeting, I modeled this strategy with two other diverse texts—*One Crazy Summer* by Rita Williams-Garcia (2010) and *Where the Mountain Meets the Moon* by Grace Lin (2009). After all of these discussions, the class developed a strong awareness of what making connections looks like and why it's an important tool for understanding all texts they encounter.

Middle-School Connection

As my eighth graders entered the room at the beginning of class, I stood at the front of the room, holding a book. "Today," I explained to them, "we're going to build off of the work we've done in our past two classes on making inferences. But instead of me talking about what inferences are and why they're important, I'm going to show you some examples of inferences I make when I read so that you can see what doing this looks like in action. For this activity," I continued, "I'm going to begin by using Sherman Alexie's (2007) book *The Absolutely True Diary of a Part-Time Indian*. This book describes a boy named Junior who lives on a Spokane Indian Reservation. He decides to leave his school on the reservation to go instead to a school where he is the only Indian student. He deals with and overcomes a lot of challenges, learning a great deal about himself in the process."

I then identified a specific passage from the book that led me to make an inference about Junior: "One excerpt from the book that really stands out to me in terms of making inferences is this one, from early in the book, in which Junior is talking about his interest in drawing: 'I think the world is a series of broken dams and floods, and my cartoons are tiny little lifeboats' (p. 6). From this sentence, I can infer that Junior is an optimistic person despite difficulties he has had to face in his life. The passage doesn't directly say this information, but I can infer from Junior's statement about his cartoons that he looks for reasons to be optimistic and hopeful in a challenging world."

Next, I shared an excerpt from the book that led me to make an inference about Junior's relationship with his dog: "Another passage that helped make an inference about Junior was this one I'm going to share with you now," I told the students, "where he's talking about his dog Oscar. In this section, Oscar is very sick and Junior is describing what he did in response to his dog's sickness: 'There was nothing I could do to save Oscar. Nothing. Nothing. Nothing. So I lay down on the floor beside him and patted his head and whispered his name for *hours*'" (p. 10). From this passage, I can infer Junior's strong love for Oscar and that this love shows itself in Junior's desire to do anything he can to make Oscar feel better. Even though Junior says—and repeats—that there was nothing he could actually do to help his dog, he still lay next to him for hours, patting his head and whispering his name. The author of this book, Sherman Alexie, doesn't have Junior say 'I love Oscar.' Instead, he describes Junior's actions that let us readers infer this."

I wrap up this discussion with a final point about making inferences: "In every book you read, you'll find inferences you can make about characters and situations the author describes. You'll use the evidence you find in the text to reach your own inferences about emotions, attributes, and other related information. In our next meeting, I'll share some inferences I made about the characters in another great book, *Amal Unbound* by Aisha Saeed (2018). After that, you'll try this strategy out in your own reading!"

High-School Connection

"We've been talking lately about the reading strategy of identifying how an author's word choice relates to the mood in a piece of writing," I began class by telling my tenth graders, "but today we're going to take that conversation further. I'm going to share with you some passages from a really powerful book that I know many of you have read: *All-American Boys* by Jason Reynolds and Brendan Kiely (2015). I'll project those passages to the front of the room with the document camera and then model how I identify aspects of the authors' word choice that significantly impact the piece's mood."

First, I displayed the following passage, which is told from the point of view of the character Rashad and describes his experience being detained after he was accused of shoplifting:

> There was blood pooling in my mouth—tasted like metal. There were tears pooling in my eyes. I could see someone looking at me, quickly fading into a watery blur. Everything was sideways. Wrong. My ears were clogged, plugged by the pressure. All I could make out was the washed-out grunts of the man leaning over me, hurting me, telling me to stop fighting, even though I wasn't fighting, and then the piercing sound of sirens pulling up. (p. 23)

I read the passage out loud and then shared my ideas: "I think the author of this passage is really effective at creating a mood of desperation. Through the word choice here, we can really get a sense of how desperate the situation is for Rashad and how helpless he feels. For example, the repetition of the verb 'pooling' in the first two sentences to describe Rashad's blood and tears sends a message that these bodily fluids are accumulating and he is unable to do anything about it. Another good example of word choice that creates this mood is Rashad's description of 'the man leaning over me, hurting me, tell me to stop fighting, even though I wasn't fighting.' Rashad's statements in this passage—such as the details about the man leaning over and hurting him and the information about being told to stop fighting even though he wasn't—contribute to the feeling of helplessness in this passage. The word choice employed by the author creates this mood for us as readers."

Next, I projected another section from the novel to the front of the room. "This is a very different passage with a different kind of mood," I explained. "In this excerpt, the book's other main character, Quinn, describes his observations of his younger brother Willy."

> He was too old to act like a frigging wild animal, but he was the baby of the family and we still treated him like one. He was in the living room with the PlayStation. His life's major achievement was the mastery of all games and how quickly he beat them. His latest was the new version of Grand Theft Auto. Ma hated the

game, but when Willy agreed to play soccer, the deal he cut, the little prince, was that he could play GTA as often as he wanted. (p. 25)

"The author's word choice in this passage conveys a mood of frustration," I asserted. "Quinn's descriptions of Willy express his frustration toward his younger brother. For example, Quinn's statement that that the family 'still treated' Willy like 'the baby of the family' expresses this frustration, as does his comment that Willy's 'life's major achievement was the mastery of all games and how quickly he beat them.' Another example of word choice that conveys this frustration is the description of Willy as 'the little prince' in the final sentence of this passage. All of these language selections contribute to the mood of frustration that exists in this section. Without these descriptions, we wouldn't be able to pick up on this mood as clearly as we can."

"These passages from *All-American Boys*," I concluded, "have very different moods, and those moods—one of helplessness and one of frustration—extend from the authors' word choice. If the authors of these passages used different language, or just chose not to use some of the descriptive terminology we identified in our discussion, we wouldn't be able to identify the moods as clearly as we currently can. We'll explore how the authors of some other books use word choice to create the moods in their pieces as well, and then I'll ask you to try this strategy out in your own readings!"

Step Four: Help Students Apply the Focal Concept to a Text of their Choice

This stage of the instructional process provides an opportunity for students to put what they've learned in the first three steps into action in their own reading by applying the strategy you've presented, explained, and demonstrated to them. To do help students this, I provide them with a graphic organizer to help them structure their thoughts while using the reading strategy. Then, I ask them to apply the strategy to their independent reading books and confer with them while doing so. The grade-level-specific connections in this section depict the graphic organizers I used with my students, as well as descriptions of individual conferences I had with students as they put these strategies into action while reading.

Elementary-School Connection

"Today's the day!" I greet my fifth graders. "We've been talking a lot about making connections lately—today's when you'll put this strategy into action in our reading workshop time using your independent reading books." I motion to the front of the room and continue: "You can see that I've projected a graphic organizer on the document camera—I'm going to ask you to use this organizer to document the connections you make when you read." (This graphic organizer is depicted in Figure 3.1 and available in reproducible form in Appendix B.)

Figure 3.1 Making Connections Graphic Organizer

Your name:

Book you're reading:

Connection type	Connection you made	Explanation of the connection
Text-to-text		
Text-to-self		
Text-to-world		

"This graphic organizer lists the three connection types—text-to-text, text-to-self, and text-to-world," I tell the students. "Next to each type, you'll list a specific connection and then explain why that's an example of a connection. For example, when I modeled connections I made when reading *Brown Girl Dreaming*, I made a text-to-text connection between Jacqueline Woodson's description of her father's football skill and a *Sports Illustrated* article about the talents of NFL running back Saquon Barkley. If I filled out this organizer, I would go to 'Text-to-text' under connection type and then write 'I compared Jacqueline Woodson's description of her father's football skill with information in a *Sports Illustrated* article about Saquon Barkley.' Then, I'd move to 'Explanation of the connection' and write why I made this connection. For this example, I'd write 'Both Woodson's father and Barkley are described as being really talented at football. These two texts are similar because of how they praise these players' skills.'

"Now," I informed the students, "it's your turn. I'll give each of you a copy of the graphic organizer; you'll use that to document the connections you make when reading your independent reading book. After you take some time to get started, I'll come around and check in to see what kinds of connections you're making." I sat down next to a young man who is reading the book *Wonder* by R. J. Palacio (2012). He explained to me that his experience with that book was full of connections. He made a text-to-self connection because the book encouraged him to reflect on times when he was in situations where people weren't being accepted, a text-to-text connection to the book *Freak the Mighty* by Rodman Philbrick (1993) because, he explained, both have to do with students who are thought of by some as different and the friendships those students make, and a text-to-world connection to bullying. These connections showed me that this student had done a great job using this strategy!

Middle-School Connection
"I'm really excited to see you all put the reading strategy of making inferences into action," I told my eighth graders. "Before you start, though, I want to share with you a graphic organizer that can help you make inferences while reading your independent reading books. As you'll see, it contains places to record inferences you make, the evidence for the inference, and an explanation of how that evidence led you to make the inference you did." I project the graphic organizer, depicted in Figure 3.2 and available in Appendix B, to the front of the room and give each student a hard copy.

"Remember how I shared some examples of inferences I made while reading *The Absolutely True Diary of a Part-Time Indian*?" I asked the students. "You may recall that one inference I shared was that Junior is an optimistic person. The textual evidence I cited for that inference is his statement 'I think the world is a series of broken dams and floods, and my cartoons are tiny little lifeboats' (p. 6). If I was filling out this graphic organizer, I would write 'Junior is optimistic' under 'An inference you

Figure 3.2 Inferences Graphic Organizer

Your name:

Book you're reading:

An inference you made	Textual evidence for that inference	Explanation of how the textual evidence led you to make that inference

made.' Then, I would write the line from the book where the graphic organizer asks for textual evidence. Finally, in the section on the graphic organizer that asks for an explanation of how the textual evidence looks for the inference, I would write 'This sentence led me to this inference because it suggests that Junior has had difficulties in life, but he still believes that good things can happen despite those difficulties.'"

"In your independent reading work today," I continued, "you'll do the same thing. As you read, try to make three inferences about a character or a situation in your book. Be sure to find specific evidence to support the inference and to explain how the evidence led you to the inference. As you work, I'll check in with you individually and see how you're doing."

The students got to work quickly, devouring their independent reading books and recording their inferences. After some time passed, I sat down with a student to get her thoughts on how she was using the strategy. She shared, "I'm reading the book *Refugee* (Gratz, 2017). A person I made an inference about is called Papa. He's the father in a Jewish family in Nazi Germany. My inference is that he is really committed to his family's safety. The part of the book that showed me this is this paragraph here that describes Papa telling his family how important it is that they get on a boat that will take them away from Nazi Germany." She pointed to a paragraph on page 37 that reads "'On the count of three, we make a break for it,' he told his family. 'Don't stop. Don't stop for *anything*. We *have* to get on that ship. Are you ready? One. Two. *Three*'." The student then explained how this excerpt led her to make this inference: "This part of the book showed me that Papa's really committed to his family's safety because of how determined he is that the family gets on the ship. He doesn't just tell them to do it. He tells them with a ton of emphasis that shows how serious he is about it."

High-School Connection

I began a recent English class with my tenth graders by telling them that they would be spending the day using the reading strategy we had been learning our previous few meetings: "Today, you'll use your independent reading books and apply the strategy we've been talking about lately of identifying the mood in a piece of writing based on the author's word choice. You've done a great job of listening and learning as I've explained and modeled this reading strategy, and today you get to put it into action on your own."

"Before you do this" I continue, "I'm going to give you a graphic organizer to help you structure your thinking and use this strategy. This organizer asks you to identify a mood you believe the author creates at some point in the book, note specific language choices she or he uses to create this mood, and record your thoughts on how these language choices create the mood. By doing all of these things, you'll record your uses of the strategy and explain your thought process as well."

I project an example of the graphic organizer—depicted in Figure 3.3 and available in Appendix B to the front of the room—and give each student a hard copy.

Figure 3.3 Mood Graphic Organizer

Your name:

Book you're reading:

Mood the author creates	Language the author uses to create the mood	Why you believe these language choices create the mood

"For example," I explain, "when I modeled this reading strategy with *All-American Boys*, I talked about how the author of one of the sections creates a mood of desperation when describing Rashad's experience being detained after he was accused of shoplifting. If I was filling out this graphic organizer, I would write 'desperation' under the heading 'Mood the author creates.' Then, under the heading 'Language the author uses to create the mood,' I would write language that stands out to me from the passage because of the desperation it expresses, like 'blood pooling in my mouth,' 'tears pooling in my eyes,' and 'the man leaning over me, hurting me, tell me to stop fighting, even though I wasn't fighting.' Finally, under the heading 'Why you believe these language choices create the mood,' I would write, 'These language choices express Rashad's helplessness desperation. They show his pain, his sadness, and the way he was treated by another person who had power over him."

"Now, it's your turn to identify the mood in the book you're reading," I told the students. "After you read for a bit, I'll begin checking in with you and talking with you about what kind of mood you're noticing in the book you're reading and what word choice helped you make that decision."

I met with a student who was reading the book *I Am Not Your Perfect Mexican Daughter* (Sanchez, 2017). "I picked up on a mood of negativity," she explained. "I'm still in the early part of the book, but so far, Julia, the book's narrator, expresses a lot of negativity towards the world, which makes sense because her sister has just died. One example of this is when Julia is eating at a diner and she goes into detail about how bad the food is. She says the coffee 'tastes as if they boiled old socks and dumped the liquid into a coffeepot.' Later in the paragraph, she says, 'And the Danish is stale, of course. I should have seen that coming'" (p. 39).

"Great job of identifying the mood and those examples of word choice," I responded. "Now, talk to me about the last item on the graphic organizer: why do you believe these language choices create this mood?"

"I think they create this mood," the student answered, "because they show that her negative attitude. When she complains about the food, she's also showing her negative attitude in general. Someone with a more positive attitude about life in general wouldn't take so much time to make negative comments about the food at a diner. They might just say, 'That wasn't great,' and then get on with their day. She really focuses on it."

"That's a really thoughtful and insightful response," I replied. "I'm really impressed with how carefully you thought about Julia's word choice and how it conveys her attitude about the world. Really nice job!"

Step Five: Ask Students to Reflect on How the Strategy Helped Them Make Sense of What They Read

In this final step of the instructional process, students think about how using the focal strategy helped them as readers. To facilitate the students' work on this activity, I provide them with reflection questions that ask them to consider how the reading strategy we focused on enhanced their reading experiences and how those experiences would have been different if they hadn't used that strategy. In this section, we'll take a look at the specific reflection questions I posed to my students and some of their responses regarding how the strategies on which they focused maximized their effectiveness as readers.

Elementary-School Connection

I greet my fifth graders by praising the work they did the previous day and introducing today's topic: "Yesterday, you all did such a wonderful job of making connections when reading your independent reading book. Today, I'm going to ask you to reflect on how making connections helped you understand what you read. To get started doing so, please take a minute and write your responses to two questions." I project two questions on the document camera: "How did making connections help you understand what you read?" and "How would your reading experience be different if you didn't make connections while reading?"

I asked the students to respond to these questions individually and then tell their thoughts to a partner. After that, I asked for volunteers to share their insights with the whole group. One student provided the especially insightful response that "Making connections helped me read because it made me pay attention to everything in the book in order to see what in the book related to either my life, another text, or the world. My reading experience would be different if I didn't make connections because I would have paid as much attention to all of the things in the book. I probably would have read it quickly to get through it." This student's comments stood out to me because of his awareness of the impact this strategy had on his reading and his understanding of how using the strategy enhanced his reading experience.

Middle-School Connection

"I'm so impressed by the great work you've been doing with making inferences," I praised my eighth graders. "You were focused and attentive in our earlier classes when I introduced and explained the concept, and then last class you very nicely applied this strategy to the books you're reading independently."

"Today," I continued, "I'm going to ask you to do something different: you're going to reflect on how making inferences helped you as a reader. I'm going to put two questions up on the document camera;

your job is to write down your answers to these questions and share them with a partner. Then, I'll ask for any volunteers who would like to share your insights with the whole class." The questions I projected to the front of the room were, "How did making inferences while reading help you comprehend the material you read?" and "How would your reading experience be different if you didn't make inferences while you were reading?"

Several students volunteered to share their ideas with the rest of the class; one responded to the first question by saying, "Making inferences helped me comprehend the material I read because, to make inferences about the characters in my book, I had to first understand what they were doing." She then commented on the second question, explaining that making inferences improved her in-depth understanding of the text: "If I didn't make inferences, I probably wouldn't have as much of an understanding of the characters because I wouldn't have spent so much time thinking about what their character traits are and how the evidence in the text helped me figure that information out." I was impressed by this student's awareness of how making inferences while reading enhanced her comprehension skills and her ability to think deeply about the material she read.

High-School Connection

I posted two questions at the front of the classroom for my tenth graders to see as they entered the room: "How did using the reading strategy of identifying the mood created by the author's word choice help you understand what you read?" and "How would your reading experience be different if you didn't use this strategy?" Once the students had a chance to read the questions, I commented further: "As you know, we've been working a lot lately on identifying the mood created by an author's word choice. I love all of the great work you all have done on this topic, especially how thoughtful and insightful you were when you applied the strategy to your independent reading books in our last class. Today, we're going to do something different with this strategy: instead of using it while we read, we're going to reflect on its importance to effective reading."

The students wrote their responses to the reflection questions. After they shared with partners, I asked for volunteers to do so with the rest of the class. One student responded to the question of how the strategy helped him understand what he read: "It helped me understand the book a lot because it made me think about the exact words the author used and why she used those words, like what mood the words were supposed to create." In reply to the question of how his reading experience would be different if he didn't use the strategy, the student explained, "I wouldn't have thought so carefully about what choices the author made and why."

These reflections convey the impact of identifying the mood in a text on the student's experience, as well as his metacognitive awareness of this strategy' impact.

Key Points about Applying Reading Strategies to Texts that Represent Diverse Backgrounds

- In this instructional practice, teachers and students apply strategies essential to effective reading—such as making connections, creating inferences, analyzing word choice, asking questions, summarizing, and forming predictions—to texts that represent a wide range of backgrounds, cultures, and experiences.
- The application of reading strategies to texts that represent diverse backgrounds, experiences, and identities helps build a culturally relevant and inclusive classroom environment in two key ways: it can help students see themselves reflected in the curriculum and can give students opportunities to learn about others' cultures and experiences; Bishop (1990) describes these benefits as "mirrors" and "windows."
  - Many texts taught in schools represent limited perspectives (Tschida, Ryan, & Ticknor, 2014); when all students see themselves reflected in the curriculum, the result is an inclusive, culturally sensitive environment that maximizes student motivation (Kumar, Zusho, & Bondie, 2018).
  - In addition, studying a diverse range of texts doesn't just benefit the students who are directly represented in those books: it can enhance the learning experiences of all students by helping learn about other cultures and experiences.
- I recommend using a five-step instructional process when helping your students apply reading strategies to a diverse range of texts:
  - Introduce a reading strategy to students.
  - Explain why the concept is important to effective reading.
  - Model the strategy by applying it to a diverse range of texts.
  - Help students apply the focal concept to a text of their choice.
  - Ask students to reflect on how the strategy helped them make sense of the text they read.

4

Using Reading Strategies in Out-of-School Contexts

In this chapter, we'll consider a culturally relevant approach to teaching our students reading strategies that calls for students to apply the reading strategies they learn in school to out-of-school situations. First, we'll examine the key components and features of this approach. Then, we'll reflect on it can be beneficial to our students. After that, I'll describe an instructional process that you can use when putting this idea into action with your students, including examples of how I implemented it with fifth-, eighth-, and tenth-grade students. Finally, I'll share some final points about the ideas presented in this chapter to consider for your future instruction.

What Is It?

In this instructional practice, teachers help students identify opportunities to apply reading strategies to out-of-school contexts. This instructional approach is based on the idea that the reading strategies students learn in school—such as the tactics of making connections, forming inferences, analyzing the effect of word choice on mood, all of which are described in the preceding chapter—are applicable to more than just school-based reading: they can be used to make sense of a range of situations that students (and all other people) encounter in their out-of-school lives. By out-of-school contexts, I mean any language-oriented event in students' out-of-school lives: this includes reading a book, poem, play, or article of one's own choice, but also extends to wider-ranging formats, such as a song, television show, film, text message, social media post, or conversation. All of these events are potential opportunities for students to apply the reading strategies they learn in school.

How Can It Help Students?

This instructional process is motivational, engaging, and academically useful; it reconceptualizes what reading strategy can look like by giving relevant and meaningful opportunities to utilize reading strategies they learn in school. In this section, we'll look closely at three key benefits: it provides students with authentic applications of academic strategies, it makes space for students' perspectives and identities, and it creates opportunities for additional uses of skills they learn in school. Let's consider each of these ideas further.

It Provides Students with Authentic Applications of Academic Strategies

The opportunity for students to apply what they learn in school to authentic contexts and situations is a key component of effective instruction, as it increases motivation and enhances student learning (Mims, 2003). Ferlazzo (2105) calls this application a transfer of learning, explaining that students develop deeper and more effective understandings of information they learn in school when they understand how to transfer that information to a variety of situations. The instructional practice of students applying reading strategies to out-of-school texts achieves these benefits by giving students a real-world use of these strategies. For example, when students apply the strategy of analyzing the impact of an author's word choice to a popular song, they will use it in an authentic, real-word setting, transferring a skill they learned in school to texts they are motivated to understand. This real-world application shows students that the strategies, skills, and ideas they learn in school don't just end when school does; instead, it shows them that these strategies are tools they can apply to the world around them, using them to make sense of all kinds of texts. When we teachers give our students opportunities to transfer their learning to other contexts, they can further grasp the usefulness of what they learn to other aspects of their lives.

It Makes Space for Students' Perspectives and Identities

In addition to providing students with opportunities for authentic application, this instructional practice facilitates the inclusion of students' individual perspectives, identities, and backgrounds. While students are able to bring their home lives into the classroom to an extent when they're allowed to choose the books they read, the opportunity to connect in-school strategies to a range of out-of-school texts provides even more benefits by giving students a wider range of ways to bring their interests and identities into the classroom. This practice further increases the relevance of students' learning and helps them feel that their unique perspectives are valued in school. An eighth grader recently shared with me that he loved the opportunity to apply the strategy of making inferences to out-of-school texts and situations because of the opportunity it gave him to bring his interests into the classroom: "I loved how you let us make inferences about a bunch of different things, not just the books here in school. It was fun for me because I made inferences about T'Challa [the film's protagonist] in *Black Panther*. I got to talk about something I love—that's my favorite movie—and could still do it while learning for school!"

It Creates Opportunities for Additional Uses of Skills Students Learn in School

The final benefit I'd like to highlight is that applying reading strategies to out-of-school texts creates more opportunities for students to use these strategies than they would otherwise have: when students learn that they can use the strategies they learn in school to make sense of material they encounter in their out-of-school lives, the number of possible situations for them to use these skills grows significantly. If students only feel that they can use the strategies they learn in school to understand school-oriented texts, they will only apply those tools to the material they encounter in school. However, if students understand that they can use strategies such as making connections, creating inferences, and analyzing word choice to make sense of songs, films, television shows, social media posts, and other texts that are relevant to their lives, they will use those strategies much more frequently. I recently spoke with a tenth grader who explained that she used the reading strategy of analyzing how authors create mood through word choice much more now that she understands how it can be applied in out-of-school contexts: "Now, I think about [this strategy] when I look at social media, like what people write on Facebook and Twitter. I think about what mood and tone they're trying to create, like if they're excited, proud, or sad about something, and what words they used to do that. Before now, I never would have thought to analyze social media like this."

How Can It Look in Action?

When I help students apply the reading strategies they learn in school to out-of-school contexts, I select a strategy that I've already taught my students using the instructional procedure described in Chapter 3. Once I've selected this strategy, I use a four-step instructional process. First, I talk with the students about how this strategy can be applied to out-of-school texts. After that, I model my own application of this strategy to a text that is relevant to my out-of-school life. Next, I ask my students to apply the strategy to out-of-school texts of their own choice. Finally, I have students reflect on how the strategy helped them make sense of the texts to which they applied it. This instructional process builds on strategies students have already learned and reconceptualizes their uses and possibilities in engaging, culturally relevant ways. It gradually releases responsibility to students, as it begins with explanation and then moves to modeling, application, and reflection. Now, let's look at each of the steps of this process in detail.

Step One: Discuss How a Reading Strategy Can Be Applied to Out-of-School Texts
This first step helps students understand how reading strategies they've learned in school can also be used to make sense of texts they encounter in other situations; it puts them in the frame of mind necessary to transfer these skills to out-of-school contexts. I've found that this instructional step is especially useful for students who have never used strategies they've learned in school in culturally relevant ways. A tenth grader recently shared with me that he had only used the reading and thinking strategies he'd learned in school to interpret school-based texts and that he benefited from how I introduced this new application: "I had never thought about texts from outside of school this way, so I was glad you explained it the way you did." When I introduce this instructional approach, I begin by reminding them of our work with the strategy and then discuss with them how it can be used to make sense of a variety of texts. This activates students' prior knowledge and prepares them to apply the skill to new situations. Now, let's take a look at how I discussed this concept with my elementary-, middle-, and high-school students.

Elementary-School Connection
My fifth graders recently entered the classroom to find the following text written on a piece of chart paper: "Making Connections: The Remix." Some students looked at me quizzically, while others smiled at my attempt to use current language, and I continued: "As you know, we've been working a lot lately with the reading strategy of making connections. Our work has been focused on applying the strategy to a wide range of books, which has been great. However, today, we're going to make our use of this strategy even more wide-ranging: we're going to think about how we can apply it to texts we read outside of school. First, let's think about what the word 'text' can mean: it be a book, a poem, or article, but it can also be anything else that involves language, like a song, movie, television show, conversation, or text message." After explaining that idea, I wrote those potential text types on the chart paper around the previously-written "Making Connections: The Remix." "This strategy," I continued, "is something that can help you understand all kinds of texts. Even though it's something you learn in school, it has a ton of applicability to your

out-of-school life also. For example, you might listen to a song and make a text-to-text, text-to-self, and text-to-world connection—all of those connections can help you understand the song, just like how doing so can help you comprehend a novel you read in school. We're going to be applying this strategy to texts you encounter out-of-school—I can't wait to see your great work!"

Middle-School Connection
On a Monday morning when my eighth graders seemed a bit sluggish, I perked them up with a real-world connection: "Have you ever watched a television show or a movie and thought about the characters' personality traits?"

"Yeah," responded a student. "I was watching [the television show] *Blackish* and thought about what the characters were like and how I could tell they were like that."

"I did that too when I watched *Jumanji: Welcome to the Jungle* a little while back," answered another. "The characters in that movie have really different personalities and I was thinking about what their traits were."

"Those are fantastic connections!" I exclaimed. "What you're both describing is the action of making inferences. We've been talking in class about how we make inferences when we read—and, as we've discussed, it's an essential aspect of effective reading. It's also important to know, though, that making inferences is something we do to make sense of all kinds of texts we interact with in our lives." I continued to explain to the students the many kinds of written texts that facilitate inferences, noting that, in addition to making inferences while reading books, articles, and poems, we also do so when we participate in conversations, watch films and shows, read interviews with celebrities, and communicate with others via text message and social media. "In our upcoming classes," I stated, "we're going to apply the strategy of making inferences to texts from your out-of-school lives. In our next meeting, I'll model an example of this—then, you'll try it out on your own!"

High-School Connection
I began a conversation with my tenth graders by praising the great work they had done with the reading strategy of identifying the mood created by an author's word choice: "You all did such wonderful work with that strategy. I loved how insightfully you applied it to your independent reading books and how you reflected on its impact on your reading." In then transitioned to that day's focus: "Today, we're going to do something different: we're going to start thinking about how we can apply the reading strategy of identifying the mood an author creates through word choice to texts you engage with outside of school. These out-of-school texts can take a wide range of forms: they can be things like books, articles, and poems, but they can also be song lyrics, conversations, social media

posts, language used in films and television shows, sports broadcasts, and really anything else that uses language."

"So, we're going to use that strategy on these other kinds of things?" a student asked.

"That's right," I responded. "I'm going to ask you to apply the strategy of identifying the mood an author creates through word choice to a text you interact with outside of school. I'm going to show you an example of this in tomorrow's class and then I'll ask you to use this strategy to help you understand and analyze a text that's relevant to you."

"That's awesome," an excited student interjected. "I love that we can bring in material that we're interested in and analyze it."

"I'm thrilled that you're so excited," I replied. "I can't wait to see the great work that you all do with this."

Step Two: Model How a Reading Strategy Can Be Applied to an Out-of-School Text

This second stage of the instructional process builds on the introductory information in the first step by providing students with an example of what applying a reading strategy to an out-of-school text looks like in action. In addition to providing students with a clear model, this step of the process is a great way for teachers to bring an aspect of their out-of-school lives into the classroom, which can help build an inclusive classroom environment. However, it's also important to note that students might look at your example to see what the "right" kind of out-of-school text to use is. To address this potential issue, I emphasize that the text I'm bringing in is something that represents my out-of-school interests, but it's not meant to tell the students what they should or should not use for their examples when they do the activity. Their examples, I tell them, will represent their lives and interests, just as mine do. When I model this practice, I describe the text I used, how I applied the strategy on which the class is focusing to that text, and how the strategy helped me understand the text.

Elementary-School Connection

"In our last class," I began a discussion by reminding my fifth graders, "we talked about applying the strategy of making connections to texts that represent our out-of-school lives. Today, I'm going to show an example of what this can look like with a text that shows my out-of-school life and interests. This will give you an example that you can draw from when you do this same thing on your own with texts of your choosing, which you'll be doing soon!"

"The text I picked," I continued, "is the animated Disney movie *Zootopia*. I've seen it few times with my youngest son and I know many of you have seen as well. I picked it because I really like the film and because I made a lot of different kinds of connections to it when I watched it. In this movie, a rabbit named Judy Hopps leaves her small town to pursue her dream of becoming a police officer in the big city of Zootopia. She meets a fox named Nick Wilde who at first is a con artist who makes her life difficult. Eventually, though, Judy and Nick work together to reveal some behind-the-scenes corruption."

"The first connection that I made," I explained, "is a text-to-self connection: I connected to the way Judy wanted to move to the big city of Zootopia because it reminded me of how much I wanted to move to New York City when I was younger. I was always fascinated by New York and saw it as a place of possibility and excitement, just like Judy saw Zootopia. Judy and I both moved to our dream destinations!" Several students laughed, and I continued, "Next, I made a text-to-text connection to the book *The City of Ember* by Jeanne DuPrau (2003). In this book, two friends named Lina and Doon work together to find and expose major conspiracies and crimes that powerful people in their city have kept hidden. While there are definitely differences in the texts, they possess the key similarities of friends working to expose corruption and conspiracies created by powerful people in their cities. Finally, I want to talk with you about a text-to-world connection that I made to *Zootopia*: many of the characters in the movie discount Judy's abilities to be a successful big-city police officer because she's a rabbit. They don't acknowledge her potential, yet she still becomes successful. This happens a lot in the real world: people are sometimes overlooked or discounted for one reason or another, but they still are able to succeed. Everyone in the world can learn from this film and give others fair opportunities to reach their goals."

I wrapped up the mini-lesson with a final comment on the importance of this strategy: "Making connections definitely helped me engage actively with the film *Zootopia* and understand it on a deeper level than if I didn't make those connections. Because I made text-to-self, text, and world connections to the film, I thought carefully about some its major issues. If I didn't make these connections, I would have still enjoyed the movie, but I wouldn't have thought as carefully about it."

Middle-School Connection
"Making inferences isn't just a strategy you use in school," I began a conversation with my eighth graders. "It's an important strategy for understanding all kinds of texts, no matter what they are. Today, I'm going to model for you an example of how I made an inference when engaging with a text outside of school."

I told the students that the text I chose to use was an interview that basketball player LeBron James conducted in 2017 with Mark Anthony Green from *GQ* magazine. "I heard some highlights of this interview with LeBron James on television," I told the students, "and I thought the comments he made were really interesting, so I looked up the whole interview. When I read LeBron's comments, I made one particularly strong inference about him: that he's really concerned with having a positive impact on society and being known for more than just playing basketball. He wants to make a difference in the world."

"There are a lot of statements LeBron makes in this interview that led me to make this inference. For example, he said 'I believe that I was put here for a higher cause' (Green, 2017, n.p.). Also, at another point in the interview, he was asked why speaking up on social issues is so important to him; he answered, 'I do it because it's my responsibility' (Green, 2017, n.p.). These statements led me to infer that LeBron wants to make a difference in the world because of the emphasis he places on having a 'higher cause' and a 'responsibility' for talking about social issues. In contrast, if he only gave interviews about basketball strategies and how many points he scored in a particular game, I would make a different inference about him: I'd probably infer that he only wanted to be seen as a basketball player."

Before I concluded the mini-lesson, I shared with the students why using the strategy of making inferences helped me understand the interview: "In this situation, I applied the strategy of making inferences to LeBron James' comments in this interview. I think it's really important to note that applying this strategy to his statements helped me understand the interview a lot better: it required me to pay attention to exactly what he was saying and to think carefully about the 'big picture' message of those comments. If I didn't use the strategy of making inferences when reading these quotes, I definitely wouldn't have focused so much on the details of his statements about what those statements help me conclude about LeBron's goals as a person. I understand him and his message really well because I applied this strategy to what LeBron James said."

High-School Connection

I recently greeted my tenth graders with a reminder of what we discussed in our previous class and an announcement of what we'd be doing that day: "Remember that in our last class we discussed applying the reading strategy of identifying the mood in a piece based on the author's word choice to texts that represent our out-of-school lives?" Students around the classroom indicate agreement and I continued: "Today, I'm going to talk with you about a way I did that with a text from my out-of-school life."

"Let me start with some context," I told the students. "I'm really into distance running—I ran track and cross country in school and have done several marathons. I, like a lot of runners, think a lot about running shoes and like to look at a catalogues and websites that advertise the latest shoes. I was looking at the website recently of a company called Brooks that makes running shoes and apparel when I noticed a statement about running in general. The statement on their site that I noticed is 'Running makes good things happen. It's the best, most addictive sport the world has ever known. It fuels confidence and optimism. It makes you feel better about yourself. It can change everything'" (Brooks, 2018, n.p.).

I further immersed students in this example by projecting the website containing it to the front of the classroom. After that, I discussed its connection to our focal strategy: "In this description, the author's word choice plays a major role in the mood that exists. The mood here is extremely positive—when I read it, I'm immediately happy that I'm a runner and I feel excited to go for my next run. This happy, positive mood is definitely a result of the word choice—the words 'confidence' and 'optimism' and statements that running 'makes you feel better about yourself' and 'can change everything' create this mood of positivity and possibility."

"If the author didn't use these words," I continued, "this would be a totally different piece with a different mood. For example, if the passage could discuss why running is good for your health using much more scientific language about what happens to your body when you run and why those things can benefit one's physical and mental health. This would still send a similar message that running is a good thing, but would have a more scientific and factual tone, instead of the extremely optimistic and excited mood that exists here in this example."

I finished this explanation with a comment on how using this strategy gave me a detailed and developed understanding of this text: "I think applying this strategy of analyzing the mood created by an author's word choice helped me make sense of this passage because it gave me the tools to look closely and carefully at what message the author was trying to get across about running and how the author actually went about getting that message across. It let me do more than just say 'This company really likes running'; it gave me a way to identify exactly what they did in the passage to show that the company thinks highly of running. This is something you can do with any text, especially those that you encounter in your out-of-school lives: you can look at the specific words that are used in a text and how those words create the mood and tone that the text's creator wants to express about the topic."

Step Three: Ask Students to Apply the Strategy to Out-of-School Texts of their Choice

This component of the instructional process transfers the ownership and responsibility of applying reading strategies to out-of-school texts to the students; it calls for students to identify a text that is relevant to them, apply the focal strategy to it, and share a summary of their analysis with the rest of the class. When I ask students to do this, I give them a graphic organizer on which to record their insights—the graphic organizers I use are depicted in this section and available in reproducible form in Appendix B. These organizers are similar to the examples depicted in Chapter 3 when the students applied the focal strategy to their independent readings books, but I still like to give them to students because they can help them structure their thoughts. Before students conduct this activity, I emphasize that they should avoid texts that can be offensive to others through their language or content. (While this has never been a problem in any of my classes, but I still like to provide a word of caution about it beforehand.) This activity allows students to incorporate relevant content of their choice into the classroom and to do so in ways that are valued academically, helping reduce the separation between school and community (Tremmel, 2006) discussed in this book's introductory section. Now, let's check out how some of my elementary-, middle-, and high-school students applied our focal strategies to texts that represent their out-of-school lives and interests.

Elementary-School Connection
"I'm so excited to talk to everyone about *Coco!*" A fifth grader recently bounded into class, excited to share how he applied the strategy of making connections to the film *Coco*, which centers around the Mexican holiday Day of the Dead and describes the experiences of a boy named Miguel who accidentally enters the Land of the Dead and discovers information that affects his family.

In the preceding class meeting, I explained to the students that they each would be applying the strategy of making connections to an out-of-school text of their choice. "You'll pick an out-of-school text and make a text-to-self, text-to-world, and text-to-text connection to it," I explained. "I'll then ask you to share your insights and analyses with the rest of the class by telling the rest of us what text you chose and what connections you made. To help you do this, I'm going to give you a graphic organizer that asks you list the text you selected and the connections you created. It will help you structure your thoughts as you apply this strategy to the text. As you can see, it's like the graphic organizer that I gave you when you made connections to an independent reading book, but this time you'll be using it as you made connections to an out-of-school text." I gave the students this graphic organizer, depicted in Figure 4.1 and available in Appendix B.

Now for the day when this student entered the classroom so excited to share his connections to *Coco*. Given his enthusiasm, he was the first in our class to discuss the connections he made to the text. "I made a text-to-self connection to the *ofrenda* [the altar containing objects that honor deceased relatives in a Day of the Dead celebration] because my family sets one of for *Día de los Muertos* also," he explained. "I made a text-to-world connection to all of the people who follow their dreams. Miguel's dream is to be a singer and he follows that dream. This is a big part of the movie and also a connection I can make to the world. The text-to-text connection I made was to the book *Family Pictures/Cuadros de Familia* (Garza, 1990) that my family has at home because that book talks about a Mexican family's traditions, like *Coco* does."

Figure 4.1 Graphic Organizer for Making Connections to an Out-of-School Text

Your name:

Out-of-school text you chose:

Connection type	Connection you made	Explanation of the connection
Text-to-text		
Text-to-self		
Text-to-world		

Middle-School Connection

I began a recent discussion with my eighth graders by explaining to them the next step of our work with making inferences and telling them how I excited I was to see what their analyses: "It's time for you all to put the strategy of making inferences into action as you examine and interpret texts that you encounter outside of school. I'm thrilled to see what you do with this! In our last class, I showed you an example of what this can look like when I made inferences about LeBron James' commitment to making a difference based on an interview he conducted with *GQ* magazine."

"When you do this on your own," I continued, "you'll want to identify some kind of text that's relevant to your out-of-school life in some way. Then, you'll use the language in that text to create some kind of evidence-based inference about an individual or situation in the text." I reminded the students of the many possible out-of-school texts they can use when applying this strategy and then introduced the graphic organizer for students to use for the activity. I projected the graphic organizer depicted in Figure 4.2 to the front of the classroom and gave each student a copy, explaining to them that this document, like the one they used

Figure 4.2 Graphic Organizer for Creating Inferences with an Out-of-School Text

Your name:

Out-of-school text you chose:

An inference you made	Textual evidence for that inference	Explanation of how the textual evidence led you to make that inference

when making inferences about their independent reading books, will help them structure their observations and analyses while applying this strategy to out-of-school texts. "In Monday's class," I told the students, referring to our next class meeting, "I'm going to ask each of you to share the out-of-school text you selected, one of the inferences you made, and what textual evidence led you to that inference."

Now, let's jump forward to the class meeting when students shared the texts they chose and inferences they made. One student chose to analyze the film *Black Panther*, making inferences about the main character based on conversations in the movie: "An inference I made about T'Challa, the main character, is that at the end of the movie he cares about helping people all over the world. A lot of the movie is about how Wakanda keeps to itself and doesn't interact with other countries. At the end of the movie, though, T'Challa and his sister Shuri are in Oakland and he tells her that she's going to be in charge of a science program there. I inferred from this that T'Challa wants to help people all over the world because he goes against how things were traditionally done in Wakanda so that he could improve the lives of other people who need help, not just Wakandans." This student's comments showed me that he applied the skills of inferential thinking to an out-of-school text by using the evidence in the film to create an inference about T'Challa's beliefs.

High-School Connection

"Okay, tenth grade English!" I enthusiastically began a class meeting. "It's time to take your skills out into the world! We've been talking a lot about identifying the mood in a piece based on the author's word choice—in our last class, I showed you an example of this from the website of a running shoe company."

"Now," I continued, "you're going to apply this strategy to an out-of-school text of your choice." I reviewed different kinds of texts that could be used for this activity, reminding students that they can apply this reading strategy to a wide range of written pieces. "No matter what kind of piece you choose, you'll want to think carefully about what kind of mood in the piece and how you feel the word choice in the piece creates that mood. Is the mood suspenseful? Excited? Joyous? Disappointed? Thankful? What words used help you make that determination? These are the kinds of questions you'll ask yourself while you work on the activity."

I gave students a copy of the graphic organizer depicted in Figure 4.3 and explained that, it, like the organizer they completed when applying this strategy to their independent reading books, would help them record and structure their insights as they looked for out-of-school texts in which the word choice contributes to the mood of the piece and analyzed the connection between the two.

Figure 4.3 Graphic Organizer for Analyzing Mood in an Out-of-School Text

Your name:

Out-of-school text you chose:

Mood created in the piece	Language used to create the mood	Why you believe these language choices create the mood

"Just like you did when you analyzed your independent reading book with this strategy in mind," I told the students, "think about the mood that's created, the language used to create the mood, and why you believe that language helps create the mood. As the graphic organizer indicates, you'll identify and analyze three examples—you can use the same out-of-school text for all three analyses or different ones." I concluded this explanation by telling the students that, in an upcoming class, they would share their analyses: "Each of you will talk to the rest of us about what you found. You'll describe an out-of-school text you chose to analyze and discuss a mood you noticed in the piece, the language used to create the mood, and why you feel those language choices create that mood."

When the students shared their observations and insights, one explanation that particularly stood out to me was a student's analysis of a conversation she heard between two of her friends: "My friends and I were talking about our school's basketball game, and one person was trying to convince the rest of us, who aren't really into sports, to go," she explained. "What I noticed was that the friend who was trying to convince the rest of us to go was using language to create a really exciting mood. She was talking about how loud the crowd gets, how much fun the cheers are, and how you get to see and talk to a bunch of people. Her language choices helped create this exciting mood because she did a good job of creating a description of the basketball game as a really fun time, even for non-sports fans. When she talked about the crowd, the cheers, and the chance to see and talk to a bunch of people, she helped the rest of us get excited about going."

Step Four: Ask Students to Reflect on How the Strategy Helped Them Make Sense of the Text to Which They Applied It

This final component of the instructional process calls for students to metacognitively think about how applying the focal strategy to an out-of-school text helped them understand it in more depth than if they hadn't done so. To facilitate these reflections, I ask students to consider how using the strategy helped them make sense of the out-of-school text they selected and how this experience differed from when they had encountered a similar text but not applied this strategy. These questions call for students to consider how using the focal strategy impacted their understanding and help them compare this experience to other times they had interacted with similar texts in their out-of-school lives. In this section, we'll consider how the elementary-, middle-, and high-school students described in this chapter responded to these reflection questions.

Elementary-School Connection

"Wonderful work yesterday!" I began a recent class with my fifth graders. "I loved hearing all of the connections you made to the out-of-school texts you identified and analyzed. Today, I'm going to ask you to reflect on how your experiences applying the reading strategy of making connections helped you understand the text you chose to work with. This is similar to what you did when you reflected on applying this strategy to your independent reading books, but this time you're going to think about the strategy with an out-of-school focus."

I projected two questions to the front of the room: "How did applying the strategy of making connections help you make sense of the out-of-school text you analyzed?" and "How would you compare this experience to the times you've encountered a similar text but didn't make connections to it?"

"I'd like you to take a few minutes and reflect on these questions," I told the students. "The first one asks you how making connections helped you understand the text you chose to analyze. For example, if you picked a song, how did applying the strategy of making connections help you make sense of that song? The second question asks you to compare your experience analyzing this out-of-school text with other times you've engaged with a similar text but not applied the strategy of making—for example, how would you compare this experience to other times you've listened to a song (or whatever type of out-of-school text you picked) without making connections to it? What was similar and what was different?"

I asked the students to write down their responses and share them with a partner; after that, I asked for volunteers to share their ideas with the rest of the class. One student explained, "I analyzed an article that gives strategies for how to play the video game *Fortnite*. Making connections helped me understand it because it made me think a lot about the information in the article. I thought about how the article related to other articles I've read, to how I already played the game, and to other kinds of advice that people give." He then compared his experience reading this article with other times he's read similar articles, asserting that he read this piece more actively than he typically does: "I read a lot of gaming guides like this, but this time was different. Making connections made me think more about the information than I usually do. I definitely understand it better because I spent so much time making connections."

Middle-School Connection

I began a class meeting with my eighth graders by commenting on the previous day's activity, in which they shared how they made inferences about out-of-school texts they analyzed: "You all did a great job of making thoughtful and insightful inferences about the out-of-school texts you selected. I loved the variety of texts you all brought in and the outstanding analyses you provided. Today, we're going to think about your work on this activity in a different way: I'm going to ask you to reflect on your experience making inferences about the out-of-school text you selected."

I displayed two reflection questions at the front of the classroom: "How did making inferences help you understand the out-of-school text you selected?" and "How would you compare this experience to times you've didn't make an inference about a similar out-of-school text?"

"For the first question," I explained, "think about the text you selected and how making inferences helped you understand it in depth. For example, if you picked a movie, reflect on how making inferences about that movie helped you understand it. For the second question, think about a time you've encountered a similar text to the one you analyzed (like a movie, song, text message, or anything else you chose) and didn't make inferences about a person or situation: how was your experience analyzing this text different from those other situations?"

I asked the students to write down some of their ideas, which they would share with a partner and then with the rest of the class if they chose. One student who chose to analyze a friend's Facebook post shared, "Making inferences about the Facebook post that I picked helped me think about and understand what the person who wrote the post was feeling when she wrote it. I looked at the words and phrases she used and inferred that she felt both happy and sad about her graduation." She compared her experience analyzing this text with other times she had read Facebook posts and not made inferences by commenting on the differences in the experiences: "I don't normally think about making inferences when I read Facebook—I just look for what's going on in people's lives. When I did this, I thought more about my friend's feelings than I usually do."

High-School Connection
"I'm really excited to hear your thoughts on the reflection questions I'm going to ask you today," I began class with my tenth graders. "You did such great work analyzing how the word choice in the out-of-school texts you selected contributed to the pieces' moods; now I'm going to ask you to reflect on the work you did and how it impacted your understanding of the texts you chose." I directed the class's attention to two reflections questions at the front of the room: "How did analyzing the connection between word choice and mood in the out-of-school text you selected help you understand that text?" and "How would you compare this experience to times you encountered a similar text but didn't apply this strategy?"

I asked the students to write their thoughts on the questions and then share those insights with a partner. After they did this, I welcomed volunteers to talk with the whole class about their reflections. One student who analyzed the connection between word choice and mood in a clothing advertisement offered her insights: "Analyzing the connection between word choice and mood helped me think about what [the text] is trying to get me to think about and feel. I picked an ad I saw online that was about summer clothes from a website. The ad used exciting and fun language to get you excited about summer and buying clothes for summer activities. When I analyzed the impact of the word choice, it was like I figured out the tactics the ad was using to get me excited." She explained that this experience was very different from other times she's encountered similar texts without using the strategy: "Normally, I don't think about the word choice and mood when I look at an ad for clothes or anything else. When I did, it was like I figured out a secret the creators of the ad were using to make me think and feel a certain way." These comments convey this student's insightful perspective on the impact this reading strategy can have; as she asserts, analyzing the mood an author creates through word choice can be like finding "a secret" the author uses so that the piece has a certain effect on the reader.

Key Points about Using Reading Strategies in Out-of-School Contexts

- In this instructional practice, teachers help students identify opportunities to apply reading strategies to out-of-school contexts.
    - By out-of-school contexts, I mean any language-oriented event in students' out-of-school lives: this includes reading a book, poem, play, or article of one's own choice, but also extends to wider-ranging formats, such as a song, television show, film, text message, social media post, or conversation.
- This instructional process can benefit students in three key ways: it provides students with authentic applications of academic strategies, it makes space for students' perspectives and identities, and it creates opportunities for additional uses of skills they learn in school.
    - The opportunity for students to apply what they learn in school to authentic contexts and situations is a key component of effective instruction, as it increases motivation and enhances student learning (Mims, 2003) through the transfer of learning from one context to another (Ferlazzo, 2015).
    - The opportunity to connect in-school strategies to a range of out-of-school texts gives students a wide range of ways to bring their interests and identities into the classroom. This practice further increases the relevance of students' learning and helps them feel that their unique perspectives are valued in school.
    - Applying reading strategies to out-of-school texts creates more opportunities for students to use these strategies than they would otherwise have: when students learn that they can use the strategies they learn in school to make sense of material they encounter in their out-of-school lives, the

number of possible situations for them to use these skills grows significantly.
- I recommend using a four-step instructional process when helping your students apply reading strategies to texts that represent their out-of-school lives:
  - Talk with the students about how a specific reading strategy they've already studied can be applied to out-of-school texts.
  - Model your own application of the focal strategy to a text that is relevant to your out-of-school life.
  - Ask students to apply the strategy to out-of-school texts of their own choice.
  - Have students reflect on how the strategy helped them make sense of the texts to which they applied it.

Section 3

Culturally Relevant Language Study

5

Considering Students' Funds of Knowledge and Language Awareness

In this chapter, we'll begin our discussion of culturally relevant language and vocabulary study. As we'll explore in more detail in this chapter and the next, language study is a wonderful opportunity for culturally relevant teaching. In this chapter, we'll first examine what students' funds of knowledge are and how they can be applied to language and vocabulary instruction. Then, we'll consider the benefits that come from incorporating funds of knowledge into language study, such as how such an approach democratizes the knowledge in a classroom and emphasizes the importance of language and vocabulary. Next, we'll look in-depth at an instructional process to use when incorporating students' funds of knowledge into language study. Finally, I'll share key ideas that can help you put the ideas discussed in this chapter into action in the classroom.

What Is It?

The term "funds of knowledge" refers to knowledge that individuals develop based on their backgrounds, cultures, interests, and experiences; it focuses on the understandings and skills that people develop based on their real-world experiences and identities (Moll & Greenberg, 1990; Gonzalez, Moll, & Amanti, 2005). Just like other components of students' home and out-of-school lives, students' funds of knowledge vary based on their individual selves. Some examples of funds of knowledge, according to research on the topic, are home language, family traditions, activities with family and friends (such as playing sports and other outings), household chores, educational activities, favorite television shows, occupations of family and community members, and scientific knowledge that is relevant to one's own life, such as understanding how and why a technological device works in the ways it does (Gonzalez, Moll, & Amanti, 2005).

In this chapter, we'll see a wide range of funds of knowledge based on students' identities, backgrounds, and interests. In the instructional approach I'll present in this chapter, students share language from their individual funds of knowledge, providing the other students in the class with opportunities to learn vocabulary terms based on their peers' backgrounds, interests, and identities. In the first step of this process, the teacher presents the concept of funds of knowledge to students. After that, students reflect on funds of knowledge important to their out-of-school lives and the language they feel is important to these topics. Then, students share with the class the funds of knowledge they each selected and the related vocabulary terms they've identified as important. Finally, students reflect on their experiences sharing their insights and hearing about their peers' knowledge.

How Can It Help Students?

This method of incorporating students' funds of knowledge can enhance students' experiences with vocabulary instruction in two key ways: 1) It democratizes the knowledge in the classroom by making vocabulary instruction relevant to students' backgrounds and 2) It emphasizes the importance of specific language and vocabulary to in-depth understandings. In this section, we'll unpack each of these benefits.

It Democratizes the Knowledge in the Classroom by Making Vocabulary Instruction Relevant to Students' Backgrounds

This instructional practice privileges students' identities, backgrounds, and cultures by calling on them to share specific examples of language that are relevant to their out-of-school lives, providing an opportunity for vocabulary instruction to incorporate student ownership. In many methods of language instruction, students are given lists of words or word parts to memorize without making any connections to their cultures or out-of-school lives. However, the diversity in students' linguistic backgrounds and experiences lends itself to culturally relevant vocabulary instruction (Souto-Manning & Martell, 2016). The approach described in this chapter gives students the opportunity to share language they use in specific aspects of their out-of-school lives.

A tenth grader with whom I recently worked explained that the opportunity to bring his own funds of knowledge into language study increased his personal connection to the curriculum: "I loved presenting to the class on the terminology used in my family's Italian traditions, like the Christmas Eve feast we have every year. It connected my culture with studying vocabulary and made me feel that I could bring in something important about me to the class." Another student in the same class contrasted this approach with her previous vocabulary instruction, highlighting the engagement she and her classmates felt when sharing language and terminology related to their out-of-school lives: "Vocab is usually really boring. We have a book and we do matching and filling-in-the-blank exercises. Talking about the vocabulary we use in our lives was really interesting and fun. I liked how we learned what our classmates' backgrounds and interests are and the language related to those things. It was much more interesting and enjoyable than the vocab books we used to use." These students' comments show how this instructional practice benefits students by incorporating their unique identities and interests into language study. As these insights suggest, vocabulary instruction can be enhanced through instructional methods that make it culturally relevant and student-centered.

It Emphasizes the Importance of Specific Language and Vocabulary to In-Depth Understandings

This instructional practice highlights the importance of using specific language and vocabulary to achieve a developed understanding of a topic. The concept of using concrete, domain-specific language that allows authors and speakers to communicate as clearly as possible is addressed in a number of standards, including the Common Core Language Standards, which call for students to use specific and clear language at the elementary-, middle-, and high-school levels (Core Standards, 2010). When students reflect and present on the specific language terms associated with their out-of-school funds of knowledge, they develop relevant understandings of the importance of concrete language to clear understandings of phenomena. In other words, just as a student would use specific terminology in a scientific report, she or he would also use concrete language when describing the vocabulary in his or her funds of knowledge. In this chapter, we'll look at examples of students identifying concrete language related to their funds of knowledge—all of the examples we'll encounter indicate the importance of clear and specific vocabulary to understanding an out-of-school concept.

How Can It Look in Action?

Now, let's take an in-depth look at an instructional process that you can use with your students to help them incorporate their funds of knowledge into vocabulary instruction. This process consists of four essential steps: 1) Introduce the idea of funds of knowledge to students, talking with them about the importance of vocabulary to understanding these topics, 2) Help students think about their own funds of knowledge and language that is important to understanding them, 3) Ask students to share with the rest of the class their funds of knowledge and key related vocabulary terms, and 4) Have students reflect on their experiences sharing language related to their funds of knowledge and listening to their peers' insights. In this section, we'll examine classroom examples of each stage of this instructional process.

Step One: Introduce the Idea of Funds of Knowledge to Students, Talking With Them About the Importance of Vocabulary to this Topic
This first step of the instructional process communicates two important concepts to students: the idea of funds of knowledge and the connection between that topic and specific vocabulary. Both of these understandings facilitate the students' success in the rest of the process since their work will require them to understand what funds of knowledge are and associated vocabulary. No matter the grade level I'm working with, I introduce these concepts by first explaining funds of knowledge and then providing examples of specific vocabulary related to one of my funds of knowledge. In recent conversations with fifth-, eighth-, and tenth-grade students, I began the conversation by writing the term "Funds of Knowledge" on a piece of chart paper and then writing a brief definition underneath, such as "Knowledge people develop based on their individual backgrounds, cultures, interests, and experiences." Next, I created a word web by drawing a circle around the term and definition and then writing different types of funds of knowledge on the lines extending from the circle. For example, when doing this with my eighth graders, I recently wrote "Family traditions, activities with friends and family, television shows and other forms of entertainment, family and community members' occupations, scientific knowledge relevant to your life."

Once I introduced this concept and these examples to my students, I introduced the importance of vocabulary to discussions of funds of knowledge: "We're going to be talking a lot about funds of knowledge in our coming classes and we're going to be thinking specifically about the vocabulary and language connected to our funds of knowledge," I told my eighth graders. "For example, one fund of knowledge for me is my background in running—I've been a runner most of my life, so it's a big part of my identity. If I were to describe that part of my identity, I would use specific vocabulary terms to discuss it in detail. I might describe specific events, such as the marathon or the 15k, or I might describe specific strategies, such as 'negative splits,' which is when you run the second half of a race faster than the second, or 'pace groups,' which is when runners who are trying to complete a race in the same amount of time run together. These vocabulary terms would help someone understand running in detail. In our next class," I continued, "we're going to talk more about the language and vocabulary related to some of the funds of knowledge in your lives."

Step Two: Help Students Think About Their Own Funds of Knowledge and Language That is Important to Understanding Them
In this second step, I like to guide the students as they reflect on their own funds of knowledge and key examples of language and vocabulary that are important to understanding those topics. To do this, I give students a graphic organizer that asks them to list a fund of knowledge

they'd like to describe, some vocabulary terms related to that fund of knowledge, and why each term is important to understanding the topic. Figure 5.1 depicts the graphic organizer I use to help students record and structure their ideas. (This document is also available in reproducible form in Appendix B.)

Figure 5.1 Graphic Organizer: Funds of Knowledge and Language

Fund of Knowledge	Key Terms Related to the Fund of Knowledge and Their Meanings	Why Each Term is Important to Understanding the Topic

I use this graphic organizer with all of the grades I teach—it provides an accessible framework for students of varying age levels to use when describing the language in a variety of funds of knowledge. Before the students begin work on this activity, I provide them with some key suggestions: "First, choose a topic that you understand well and is personally meaningful to you," I recently told a group of fifth graders. "That will help ensure that you're working with material you're interested in and you know a lot about. Next, try to pick language that's very specific and specialized to that topic. When I talked about running in our last activity, I didn't pick broad and general words like 'fast' and 'good.' I picked specific language about events and running strategies. Finally," I explain, "when you get to the last section of the chart that asks you why each term is important to understanding the topic, make a case for why it's important that people understand each term you listed. Think about why someone would need to know that word to really comprehend the details of your topic."

Before students begin work on the graphic organizer, I explain that their work on it will inform their upcoming presentations: "You're going to give a presentation to the class," I told my fifth graders, "based on the information you record on this graphic organizer. You'll share with the rest of us the topic you picked as your fund of knowledge, three or four key vocabulary terms related to that fund of knowledge, and why each term is important to understanding the fund of knowledge you selected." While students work on the graphic organizers, I hold one-on-one conferences with them, checking on their progress, making suggestions, and answering questions.

During these meetings, I ask them to tell me about their topics and the relevant language they've selected. I look to see if the language is concrete and specific enough and give suggestions if it's a bit vague or general—for example, I helped a fifth grader who worked on the topic of basketball come up with more specific words for "shot," working with him to identify specific types, such as "free-throw" and "three-pointer." Once I've talked with students about the specificity of their language, I ask them to talk with me about why each term they've listed is important to understanding the topic they've selected. (The student who identified basketball-related language discussed how the types of scoring and the different positions he identified showed the variety of ways people can play the game of basketball—such as guards can shoot a lot of three pointers, while bigger players can score more points closer to the basket.) When students can explain these components, I've confident that they're ready to present their findings in the next step of the process.

Step Three: Ask Students to Share Their Funds of Knowledge and Key Related Vocabulary Terms
Now that students have brainstormed language related to their funds of knowledge, the next step is for them to share their ideas with the rest of the class! To do this, I ask each student to prepare a brief presentation

based on the information in the graphic organizer in Figure 5.1; in these presentations, each student identifies the fund of knowledge on which she or he is presenting, defines key vocabulary terms related to that topic, and explains why each term is important to understanding the topic. These presentations are great examples of students sharing relevant information in academically oriented ways—I like to ask other teachers to bring their students to come see the presentations. Let's take a look at some examples of upper-elementary, middle-, and high-school students' ideas and insights.

Elementary-School Connection
When my fifth graders entered class on a recent Monday morning, they noticed the words "Funds of Knowledge Presentations" written on the whiteboard. "Today," I enthusiastically reminded the students, "you'll share with the rest of the class the fund of knowledge you've selected and examples of specific language associated with that fund of knowledge. You've been working hard on this and I'm excited to hear what you all have to say."

The first student to present discussed his interest in fishing, explaining that it is a tradition in his family and that he had been going fishing with his father and older brothers for as long as he has been able. "It's an important activity in our family," he asserted, "because my dad, brothers, and I have been doing it for a long time, and my dad did it with his brothers and father." The student continued to explain the vocabulary terms he identified as important to fishing: "There are some words you need to know to understand fishing. The first one I picked out is bait, which is a food you put on the end of a hook to catch a fish. The second one is lure—a lure is like bait, but it's artificial, not actual food like bait is. You use it to get a fish's attention and then hook it. Lures are usually colorful or have a fancy design to get the fish to notice it. The third word I picked out is sinker. That's a weight you use near the bait or the lure to make it sink more in the water. The last word I picked is cast, which is what you do when you throw a fishing line into the water to catch something."

This student continued to explain why each of these terms is important to understanding fishing. He noted that understanding the words lure and bait is essential because "These are the words that describe what you use to actually catch the fish. If you don't know those words," he continued, "you won't know what to use to catch fish." He explained that the term sinker is important to understanding fishing since "A sinker really helps you catch fish by making your lure or bait sink. Without it, you wouldn't catch fish as well." Finally, he explained that "Cast is an important word because you have to cast a line into the water in order to fish. That word is like a basic component of fishing." This student's identification of key fishing-related terminology and discussion of the importance of this language to understanding fishing struck me as impressive: he thought carefully about key terms and their significance to this topic.

Middle-School Connection

When my eighth graders recently presented on their funds of knowledge and key examples of language related to these topics, one student whose work stood out to me identified one of her funds of knowledge as dairy farming—her family owns and operates a dairy farm. Her detailed discussion of the vocabulary associated with dairy farming showed that a strong knowledge of the terminology associated with this practice is important to being successful in it. She explained, "You really need to know terms to be a dairy farmer."

"There are different breeds of cattle and dairy farmers need to know the differences between the breeds. For example, Holsteins are black and white cows and have the highest milk production of all dairy cows. Jersey cows are brown and produce milk with high fat and protein. You also need to know about the kinds of equipment you have on a dairy farm, like a baler, a machine that turns hay into bales that are fed to the cows, and a bulk tank, a large container where milk is kept cool."

When describing the importance of these terms to the topic of dairy farming, this student explained that it's important to know about specific breeds so that one understands their unique attributes: "Every breed, like Holsteins and Jerseys, is a little different, so you have to know about each one to know how they're different, like how much and what kind of milk they give." She also commented on the significance of knowing the names and features of equipment: "You need to know what all of the equipment is so that you know exactly what it does and can use it that way." These statements suggest that being able to use these terms effectively is essential to success as a dairy farmer; without a knowledge of these terms, it would be difficult for a farmer to function effectively.

High-School Connection

A tenth-grade student with whom I worked gave an excellent presentation on key language associated with Ramadan, a month of fasting observed by Muslims. She began by identifying Ramadan as one of her funds of knowledge, explaining, "I'm going to be observing Ramadan soon, so I decided to use language about Ramadan for this project." This student identified four terms that she felt were especially important to Ramadan: fasting, Quran (the holy book of Islam), Suhoor (the meal eaten before dawn during Ramadan), and Iftar (the meal eaten at sunset during Ramadan that ends the day's fast). After identifying and defining these terms, she explained the significance of each: "Fasting is really important—it's basically what Ramadan is about: Muslims fast without eating or drinking during daylight hours in Ramadan from dawn to sunset. The Quran is also really important to Ramadan because Muslims are encouraged to read it during the month of Ramadan. The last two words—Suhoor and Iftar—are important because those are the two meals that Muslims eat during Ramadan. That's really important to know since those things are such important parts of life during Ramadan! My dad was telling me about Muslims who get together and play soccer at night after Iftar—if someone didn't know what Iftar is, it would be hard to understand what he was talking about!" This student did a great job of identifying these key terms and explain their relevance to Ramadan. I particularly appreciated the description of the soccer games played after Iftar; it's certainly true, as this student mentions, that an understanding of this term is important to comprehending the information.

Step Four: Have Students Reflect on their Experiences with this Activity
In this final step of the instructional process, I ask students to comment on what this experience was like for them, focusing not only on them sharing language related to their funds of knowledge, but also on listening to their peers' insights. I've found that asking students to reflect on these ideas helps them consider the impact that this instructional practice has had on their understanding of the importance of vocabulary to effective communication and to their out-of-school funds of knowledge. To facilitate these insights and analyses, I ask students a reflection question that helps them consider what they learned from this instructional process: "What did you learn about the importance of vocabulary from sharing language related to one of your funds of knowledge and listening to your peers share theirs?"

I first ask students to record their thoughts on a sheet of paper and share them with a partner. After they've done this, I call for volunteers to tell their thoughts to the whole class. I recently presented this reflection question to my fifth-, eighth-, and tenth-grade class and was impressed by all of the thoughtful and insightful comments. For example, the eighth grader described in the previous section who presented on language associated with dairy farming explained, "I learned that knowing the vocabulary about something is really important to understanding it. If you don't know the key words about a topic and what they mean, like the examples I gave with dairy farming, you're not going to understand it clearly." A tenth grader shared similar insights, commenting on the importance of specific language to understanding a concept in detail: "When I listened to all my classmates talk about their funds of knowledge, I really noticed how much specific language there was and how important all that language is. Now that I know the specific language they talked about, I understand the information they shared a lot more than I did before I knew those terms." These insights, as well as others that the students in my classes shared, showed that the students understood the importance of specific language and vocabulary to clear communication, and that this activity involving funds of knowledge helped them grasp that concept.

Key Points about Considering Students' Funds of Knowledge and Language Awareness

- In this instructional practice, students share language from their individual funds of knowledge, providing the other students in the class with opportunities to learn vocabulary terms based on their peers' backgrounds, interests, and identities.
  - The term "funds of knowledge" refers to knowledge that individuals develop based on their backgrounds, cultures, interests, and experiences; it focuses on the understandings and skills that people develop based on their real-world experiences and identities (Moll & Greenberg, 1990; Gonzalez, Moll, & Amanti, 2005).
  - Some examples of funds of knowledge, according to research on the topic, are home language, family traditions, activities with family and friends (such as playing sports and other outings), household chores, educational activities, favorite television shows, occupations of family and community members, and scientific knowledge that is relevant to one's own life, such as understanding how and why a technological device works in the ways it does (Gonzalez, Moll, & Amanti, 2005).
- This method of incorporating students' funds of knowledge into vocabulary instruction can benefit students in two key ways: it democratizes the knowledge in the classroom by making vocabulary instruction relevant to students' backgrounds and it emphasizes the importance of specific language and vocabulary to in-depth understandings.
  - This practice democratizes the knowledge in the classroom because it privileges students' identities, backgrounds, and cultures by calling on them to share specific examples of language that are relevant to their out-of-school lives, providing an opportunity for vocabulary instruction to incorporate student ownership.
  - It emphasizes the importance of specific language and vocabulary to in-depth understandings by showing students that concrete, domain-specific terminology is essential to communicating effectively about their funds of knowledge.
- I recommend using a four-step instructional process when helping your students connect their funds of knowledge to the idea of specific language and vocabulary:
  - Introduce the idea of funds of knowledge to students, talking with them about the importance of vocabulary to understanding these topics.

- Help students think about their own funds of knowledge and language that is important to understanding them.
- Ask students to share with the rest of the class their funds of knowledge and key related vocabulary terms.
- Have students reflect on their experiences sharing language related to their funds of knowledge and listening to their peers' insights.

6

Connecting Linguistic Diversity to Word-Root Instruction

In this chapter, we'll continue our exploration of culturally relevant language and vocabulary instruction by examining instructional methods for teaching students word roots in ways that facilitate connections to language they use in their out-of-school lives. We'll begin by discussing what this instructional practice is, which we'll follow by considering why this process can benefit our students. After that, we'll look at an instructional process to use when putting this idea into action in your own classroom. Finally, we'll conclude with key recommendations for putting the ideas presented in this chapter into action in your classroom.

What Is It?

This practice applies the principles of culturally relevant pedagogy to word-root-based vocabulary instruction, which teaches students Greek and Latin word roots to help them broaden their vocabularies and understand the relationships between words. Figure 6.1 depicts some high-frequency word roots that teachers can use in this instructional approach. (This figure is also available in reproducible form in Appendix B.)

At the beginning of this instructional process, teachers present student with key Greek and Latin roots, explaining those roots' meanings and how they relate to other words. Next, teachers explain to students how they can connect their understandings of those roots to words related to their out-of-school lives, cultures, and linguistic backgrounds, providing them with a graphic organizer that facilitates these connections. After that, students work independently to make these connections. Then, the students share with the rest of the class the word roots they

Figure 6.1 Selected High-Frequency Greek and Latin-Based Word Roots

Root	Meaning	Used in a Word
Anti	Against	Antisocial
Arch	Most important	Archenemy
Biblio	Book	Bibliography
Bio	Life	Biology
Celer	Fast	Accelerate
Cert	Sure	Certain
Dem, Demo	People	Democracy
Ego	I	Egotistic
Extra, Extro	Beyond	Extraterrestrial
Geo	Related to the earth	Geology
Mal	Bad, wrongful	Malevolent
Max	Largest	Maximize
Mem	Mind	Memory
Nov	New	Novice
Omni	All	Omnivore
Path	Emotion	Empathy
Post	After	Postpone
Sol	Sun	Solar
Un	Opposite	Unfair
Ver	Truth	Verify

selected and the connections they made. Finally, students reflect on their experiences investigating these word roots and making relevant connections to them.

How Can It Help Students?

Giving students the opportunity to apply their knowledge of word roots in culturally relevant ways incorporates research-based best practices of vocabulary instruction, while also providing the benefits of relevance, engagement, and meaningful application that accompany culturally relevant teaching. The practice of using Greek and Latin word roots is an effective method of vocabulary instruction because it presents the prefixes, bases, and suffixes students learn as "building blocks" of language: the majority of words students encounter in academic contexts are derived from Greek and Latin roots (Padak, Newton, Rasinski, & Newton, 2008). In addition, root-based instruction is a great way to support the vocabulary development of English language learners because it helps those students make connections to words from other language that also contain words based on similar roots (Rasinski, Padak, & Newton, 2017). A lot of teachers understand that Greek and Latin roots are important to effective vocabulary instruction, but are still figuring out the best way to use them in their teaching (Rasinski, Padak, & Newton, 2017)—that's where the ideas in this chapter come in! By creating opportunities for students to find examples of these roots in words they encounter in their out-of-school lives, cultural backgrounds, and home languages, teachers can provide students with meaningful and relevant contexts for applying their knowledge of this concept. The instructional practice described in the next section will provide you with a concrete understanding of what this method can look like and the kinds of engaged and well-informed student responses it can foster.

How Can It Look in Action?

To help students learn about Greek and Latin word roots and connect their knowledge of them to language relevant to their out-of-school lives, I recommend implementing a four-step instructional process: 1) Show students key Greek and Latin words, explaining their meanings and importance, 2) Discuss with students how to connect the word roots they learn to their out-of-school lives, backgrounds, and cultures, 3) Have students share the word roots they selected and the connections they made, and 4) Ask students to reflect on their experiences with this instructional process. Let's examine each of these steps individually, looking at how I put each one into action with my students.

Step One: Show Students Key Greek and Latin Roots, Explaining Their Meanings and Importance

In this first step of the instructional process, teachers present the idea of learning vocabulary through Greek and Latin roots to their students. I begin these initial conversations by showing students the high-frequency roots in Figure 6.1 and discussing the importance of those roots: "Greek and Latin word roots like these are important building blocks of language and vocabulary," I recently told my eighth graders. "While not every word in the English language comes from a Greek or Latin root, very many do, as you can see from the examples listed on this chart. When you know a root, you're not just learning one word: you're unlocking your ability to understand a whole bunch of words that contain that root. For example, if you know the root 'mal,' you're helping yourself unlock the meaning of all of the words in language that come from that root, like malcontent, which means someone who's typically unhappy, and malevolent, which means having a desire to harm others."

When working with the fifth-, eighth-, and tenth-grade classes discussed in this book, I presented all twenty roots in Figure 6.1 to each of them because I wanted to expose them to a wide range of Greek and

Latin roots that make up key building blocks of the English language. (However, you can certainly give your students a more focused version of that list if you prefer, selecting five to ten roots that you think align with what your students are ready to learn at that time.) After I share the roots with students, I ask them to work in groups to identify additional words that contain each root and to explain how those words' meanings are related to the root's. This gives students a low-stakes way to explore the Greek and Latin roots in-depth, further developing their knowledge of the topic in a cooperative environment. The roots that students are exposed to at the beginning of this process are important for multiple reasons: they not only communicate to students that word roots are key building blocks of language study that help us understand new words and the relationships between them, but also prepare students for success in the rest of this activity, which calls for them to identify culturally relevant words that contain these roots.

Step Two: Discuss with Students How to Connect the Word Roots They Learn to Their Out-of-School Lives, Backgrounds, and Cultures
This second step infuses culturally relevant instructional methods into word-root-based language study by asking students to find words they encounter their out-of-school lives, cultural backgrounds, and home languages that use one of the focal roots. I recently explained this idea to my tenth graders by connecting to the previous day's instruction and introducing the culturally relevant extension: "Yesterday, we talked about word roots and how they represent important building blocks of language study. You all did great work talking about the roots I shared with you and identifying examples of words that contain them. Today, we're going to take our work with roots even further: I'm going to ask you to identify a word that you've encountered in your out-of-school life that uses one of these roots, reflect on its meaning, and think about why it's a good example of the root it contains."

I continued to explain the variety of contexts in which students might encounter one of these words: "There are a lot of different possibilities for identifying the out-of-school word you'll analyze. It can be from something you read outside of school, which could be in a book, an article, a social media post, a text message, or anything else. It can be something you heard in a conversation, song, film, or television show. I also want to let you that the word you identify doesn't even have to be in English: if you hear another language at home and one of those words contains a root we've studied, you're totally welcome to use that word. The really wide range of possible contexts in which you'll find these roots shows how much they're used and how much they really are building blocks of language."

To help students make these connections, I give each of them a copy of the graphic organizer depicted in Figure 6.2 (and available in Appendix B) and explain its components.

Figure 6.2 Graphic Organizer for Connecting Word Roots with Students' Out-of-School Lives, Backgrounds, and Cultures

Word root	
The root's meaning	
Word you've encountered outside of school (in English or another language) that contains this root	
Where you encountered the word	
The word's meaning	
Connection between the word and the root it contains	

When I share this organizer with students, I explain that it is designed to help them think further about how word roots represent building blocks of language: "You'll select a root from the list we looked at in class yesterday and identify its meaning," I told my tenth graders. "After that, the fun, begins! Over the next week, you'll identify a word you have encountered in your out-of-school life (either during this week or one you remember encountering previously) and record that work, where you encountered it, the word's meaning, and how that word relates to the root it contains."

Before the students began work on the activity, I shared an example I created: "When I conducted this activity, I picked the word root 'mem,' which means 'memory.' A word I encountered in my out-of-school life that contains this root is 'commemorative.' I encountered it because I ran a marathon race that advertised commemorative products for sale, like t-shirts, hats, and other running gear. According to the *Merriam-Webster Dictionary*, the word 'commemorative' means 'issued in limited quantities for a limited time to honor or feature someone or something.' The connection between this word and the root it contains is that commemorative items, like the running gear for sale at the marathon, are meant to help people remember an event—in other words, these items help keep the event in someone's memory."

I gave my fifth-, eighth-, and tenth-grade students a week to work on the graphic organizer; after that week, they would then present their roots and relevant examples with the rest of the class. I did, however, check in with all of the students during that week. Since my fifth graders needed more support staying on track, I required them to turn in drafts of their graphic organizers, on which I gave written feedback. With my eighth and tenth graders, I held one-on-one conferences in which I asked students to show me their graphic organizers and gave concrete suggestions. When giving feedback to my students on their work, I made sure that each of them understood the root he or she had selected, accurately identified a word that contained the root, and was able to express the connections between that word and the root in contained. Once my students were able to do this, I knew that they were ready to present their work!

Step Three: Have Students Share the Word Roots they Selected and the Connections they Made

Now that the students have identified word roots and found examples of words containing them in their out-of-school lives and cultures, it's time for them to present their findings to the rest of the class! To do this, I ask students to present by sharing the information on the graphic organizers they completed. Like the funds-of-knowledge language presentations described in Chapter 5, these presentations are great opportunities for students to make personal and relevant connections to language and vocabulary study; it not only allows students to share language that's meaningful to them in an academically oriented way, but also gives them a chance to hear about vocabulary that is meaningful to their peers' identities and backgrounds. Let's take a look at some examples from the fifth-, eighth-, and tenth-grade students with whom I've recently worked.

Elementary School Connection

"I can't wait for your presentations today!" I greet my fifth graders at the door as they enter the classroom. "You'll talk to the rest of us about the root you picked, its meaning, a word you've encountered outside of school that contains the root, where you encountered that word, the word's meaning, and your thoughts on the connection between the word you identified and the root it contains. I'm really excited to hear what you all found. Please take out your graphic organizers and any notes you have. Once everyone is ready, we'll take a volunteer to get us started!"

The first student to volunteer selected the root biblio: "Biblio means 'book,'" she explained. "A word I heard outside of school that contains this root is 'biblioteca,' the Spanish word for library. I heard the word when I was talking with my grandmother when she was having dinner at our house. I asked her what she did that day and she told me she went to the biblioteca to get some new books to read. My grandmother's first language is Spanish. She tries to talk to my siblings and me in English, but sometimes uses some Spanish words in mostly English sentences, like she did [in this situation]. The connection between the word 'biblioteca' and the root 'biblio' is that 'biblio' means 'book' and a biblioteca, or library, is a place you'd go to borrow a book." This student's comments especially stood out to me because of how much of her family's bilingual culture she conveyed through a discussion of the root 'biblio' and the Spanish word 'biblioteca': she not only showed excellent understanding of the content, but also provided a description of an authentic use of a word containing this root.

Middle-School Connection

"Can I go first, please?" an excited eighth grader asked on the day he and his classmates were scheduled to present the word roots they selected and the relevant words they identified.

"Absolutely," I responded, smiling. "I'm thrilled that you're so excited to share your work."

"Thanks!" the student answered, sprinting to the front of the class to give his presentation. Gathering his composure, he began, "The word root I picked is 'arch.' It means 'most important.' The word I picked out that contains this root is 'archrival.' I heard this word when I was listening to sports reporters on television talking about the Red Sox playing the Yankees over the weekend. They said that the two teams are archrivals and that they're battling for first place, so their games were meaningful for both of those reasons. 'Archrival' means someone's biggest, or most important, opponent or rival, and fits the Red Sox and Yankees perfectly—when those two teams play, they really want to beat each other! They're usually both really good, so that's part of it, but they also have a history of always playing really competitive games and not liking each other very much, so that's part of it, too! The root 'arch' and the word 'archrival' are perfectly connected because 'arch' means most important and 'rival' is an opponent, so they work together to mean someone or something's most important opponent." This student's enthusiasm for the content was impressive (I've never seen a student so excited to give a presentation!), as was his understanding of how the components of the word "archrival" work together to express its meaning. His response was full of insightful comments and relevant connections!

High School Connection
When my tenth graders recently gave their word-root presentations, a student whose work particularly stood out to me shared two related, yet distinct words that contained the root "celer," which, as she explained, "means fast or speed." She identified words she heard outside of school that contain these roots and the situation in which she encountered them: "I heard the words 'accelerate' and 'decelerate' on Saturday when my dad was teaching me to drive. We were on the road and at one point he said I should hit the gas to accelerate. At another time, when were pulling up to a line of cars waiting for a red light to turn green, he told me to use the break to decelerate. 'Accelerate' means to speed up and 'decelerate' means to slow down. Both of these words are totally related to the root 'celer' because they both relate to speed—one to increase it and one to decrease it." She continued to comment on the presence of the root in two words with opposing meanings and the additional components that impact the words' meanings: "These words literally mean the opposite thing—speed up and slow down—but they both contain the same root and are both related to speed. One starts with 'ac' and the other starts with 'de,' and they have opposite meanings because of that." I was impressed by the way this student identified two words containing this root and commented insightfully on the similarities and differences between their meaning and structure; her commentary on the prefixes that resulted in the words having opposing meanings showed that she was thinking carefully about how the components of words can impact their meanings.

Step Four: Ask Students to Reflect on their Experiences with this Instructional Process
This final step helps students reflect on what they learned from identifying and analyzing relevant words that contain key Greek and Latin roots and listening to their peers share their insights by focusing on how their experiences with this instructional process impacted their understandings of vocabulary. To guide students through these reflections, I ask them to respond to the following two-part question: "What did you learn about vocabulary by identifying and analyzing words in your out-of-school life

that contain Greek and Latin roots and listening to your peers' presentations on their experiences doing this?" This question is designed to help students reflect on how connecting the concept of Greek and Latin roots to words they encounter in their everyday lives enhanced their understanding of language, as well as how hearing about their peers' insights further broadened their understandings.

I posed this question to the fifth, eighth, and tenth-grade classes described in this chapter, asking the students in each class to record their thoughts on paper and tell them to a partner, and then for volunteers to share their insights with the rest of the class. A common theme in all of the students' responses was that the entire instructional process—the students' work on the activity and their experiences listening to their peers—revealed that Greek and Latin roots are more relevant to students' out-of-school lives than they initially expected. A fifth grader commented on the prevalence of Greek and Latin roots by explaining, "What I most learned was that the word roots you showed and explained to us are in words we see and hear all the time." An eighth-grader offered a similar insight, commenting on how his individual work combined with his classmates' presentations to show him how common Greek and Latin roots are in everyday vocabulary: "I learned that so many words come from Greek and Latin roots. I noticed this when I was paying attention to words in my everyday life that come from these roots and I also noticed it when I was listening to everyone else's presentations. It was cool seeing and hearing about all the words people shared—all the words were different, but they all came from these roots." In another thoughtful and related comment, a tenth-grade explained that she had previously understood that many words contained Greek and Latin roots, but was struck by how widely used words containing those roots are: "I knew there are a lot [of words that contain these roots], but I always thought of them as just things related to school. I learned that the words with these roots in them aren't just in vocab books or study guides or things like that. We hear [words containing Greek and Latin roots] in songs, in conversations, on Facebook, and other places. I was surprised at first when people talked about all of those examples, but it really does make sense when you think about it." These comments reveal students' insights into the importance of this concept to the construction of language and the applicability of Greek and Latin roots to words they encounter in their everyday lives.

Key Points about Connecting Linguistic Diversity to Word-Root Instruction

- ♦ In this instructional practice, students identify words they encounter in their out-of-school lives that contain Greek and Latin roots, analyze the importance of those roots to the words they select, and share their findings with their classmates.

- This method of vocabulary instruction benefits students by combining research-based best practices of vocabulary instruction with the relevance, engagement, and meaningful application that accompany culturally relevant teaching.
  - Many teachers know that Greek and Latin roots are effective tools for teaching vocabulary, but are unsure how to put this idea into action in their classrooms in meaningful ways (Rasinski, Padak, & Newton, 2017); the ideas in this chapter can solve this problem by providing a meaningful and relevant application of students' understandings of word roots.
- I recommend using a four-step instructional process to help students learn about Greek and Latin word roots and connect their knowledge of them to language relevant to their out-of-school lives:
  - Show students key Greek and Latin words, explaining their meanings and importance.
  - Discuss with students how to connect the word roots they learn to their out-of-school lives, backgrounds, and cultures.
  - Have students share the word roots they selected and the connections they made.
  - Ask students to reflect on their experiences with this instructional process.

Section 4

Putting it All Together

7

Ideas for Building an Inclusive Classroom Environment

Throughout this book, we've looked together at specific instructional practices that can make the English language arts curriculum culturally relevant: these methods will help your students make connections between the academic material they learn in your classroom and material related to their interests, backgrounds, and out-of-school lives. However, for these instructional practices to be effective, it's essential for the teacher to build an inclusive classroom environment that ensures that all students feel welcomed and valued. The feelings of support and safety that come from a welcoming and inclusive classroom environment can make students more likely to form and share connections between the information they learn in school and their out-of-school lives, which are essential aspects of culturally relevant teaching.

In this chapter, we'll look at four strategies you can use to build an inclusive classroom environment that facilitates culturally relevant teaching: 1) Incorporate diverse texts, 2) Ask students to make connections to their out-of-school lives, 3) Meet with students individually about their progress, and 4) Build in opportunities for all students to share. The discussion of each strategy is divided into two parts: "What is it?" and "How can it help build an inclusive classroom?" Let's get started with our exploration of this important topic!

Incorporate Diverse Texts

What Is It?
Teachers who incorporate diverse texts in their classroom provide students with reading materials that represent characters with diverse backgrounds, experiences, and identities. There a range of ways teachers can include

diverse texts in their classrooms, such as through the books in the classroom library, assigned texts students read, examples used in reading and writing mini-lessons, and read-aloud texts. I strongly recommend that teachers use diverse texts in all of these ways to maximize students' exposure to them and to emphasize their value in all aspects of the curriculum. For example, I recently spoke with a ninth-grade teacher who not only curated a classroom library that contained a great deal of diversity, featuring texts and authors representing a variety of cultural backgrounds, identities, and experiences, but also extended this same diversity to the books she assigned in her class—this combination provided her students with a variety of opportunities to engage with diverse texts.

How Can It Help Build an Inclusive Classroom?
Incorporating diverse texts helps build an inclusive classroom because it sends the message that all identities, cultures, and experiences are valued. When students see classroom libraries, whole-class texts, and other reading materials that represent a wide range of backgrounds, they can be more likely to think, "This classroom is a place where all people are seen as valuable and important." Chapter 3 of this book, "Applying Reading Strategies to Texts that Represent Diverse Backgrounds," explains that incorporating diverse texts helps more students see themselves reflected in the curriculum, while also helping students learn about other cultures and experiences: the combination of these two components builds an inclusive classroom environment that communicates to students that all cultures have an important role in the work done there. Conversely, when a classroom's library, assigned texts, and other materials don't provide diverse representation, students may not infer that the classroom is such an inclusive place. To help all of our students feel included and valued in the classroom, we can start by providing diverse texts that facilitate these feelings of inclusion.

Ask Students to Make Connections to their Out-Of-School Lives

What Is It?
Teachers who put this strategy into action in their classrooms ask their students to connect strategies, ideas, and concepts they learn in school to aspects of their out-of-school lives. In this book, we've looked at a number of ways to do this in the English and language arts classroom, such as applying reading and writing strategies to out-of-school texts and situations and connecting language-study principles such as specific vocabulary and word roots to students' funds of knowledge and real-world experiences. These practices develop students' academic understandings while also incorporating components of their individual identities, cultures, and experiences.

How Can It Help Build an Inclusive Classroom?

Instructional practices that connect academic content to students' out-of-school lives build inclusive classrooms by sending the message that all students' cultures, identities, and backgrounds are essential parts of the classroom environment. When we give our students opportunities to connect the English and language arts concepts they learn in school to authentic situations in their out-of-school lives, we help create a classroom environment that welcomes all literacy experiences, and, by extension all of our students. By valuing the ways in which our students apply literacy practices outside of school, we value them as individuals. After I asked the students described in Chapter 1 of this book to find examples of writing strategies in their out-of-school lives, several commented that they felt recognized and empowered: "I loved that I could bring in examples of sensory details from things from my life, like music, or a conversation I had, or something on social media," explained an eighth grader. "It made me feel like I matter because I can bring in things from my life and show that they have to do with what we're learning. I've never done that before."

Meet with Students Individually About their Progress

What Is It?

Individual meetings with students about their work and levels of progress, often called one-on-one conferences, are conversations between students and teachers that allow for the two of them to talk about a student's progress, what next steps the student should take, and how the teacher can facilitate the student's success. Typically, teachers will confer with their students during independent work time—for example, when my students are doing independent reading, I'll meet with them about their progress on the topic: we'll discuss the book the student is reading, what reading strategies the student is using to comprehend the book, and some ideas and strategies for the student to continue to consider as he or she continues to read the book. The same conference framework also applies to one-on-one writing conferences (in which the teacher and student discuss the piece of writing the study is working on, what goals the student has for the piece, and the teacher's recommendations for making the piece as strong as possible) and vocabulary study (where the teacher will confer with students about vocabulary-related projects, such as the funds of knowledge and language assignment described in Chapter 5 of this book and the word-root project described in Chapter 6). During these meetings, teachers can provide students with individualized and differentiated instruction that focuses on students' individual work and the strengths and needs that work indicates.

How Can It Help Build an Inclusive Classroom?

In addition to their academic benefits, one-on-one conferences can also help build individual relationships between teachers and students that foster a classroom environment in which all students feel known and recognized as individuals. A major benefit of holding these conferences that I've noticed when working with my students is that they give me important insights into my students' individual interests and backgrounds. Whether a student is working on a piece of writing, an independent reading book, or a language-study project, holding a conference with that individual gives me an opportunity to find out more about her or his interests, both in and out-of-school (as well as the way these in and out-of-school interests intersect). Once I have this knowledge about students' interests, I can then use this information to build relationships with my students that show I know and care about them as people. This can be done in a follow-up conference (such as showing students I remember their reading and writing interests and recommending other ways they might write about a similar topic or suggesting other texts to read that might interest them), a relevant example I use in a mini-lesson (for example, I'll often show students examples of grammatical concepts in popular culture texts in which students have expressed interest, such as relative clauses in the musical *Hamilton*), or just in brief conversations before or after class that show students I see them as individuals. Holding individual conferences with students allows me to know them much better than if I only delivered whole-class instruction; the knowledge I gain about my students and interests and backgrounds helps me form connections with them and develop the sense of community in our classroom.

Build in Opportunities for All Students to Share

What Is It?

There are a number of ways for teachers to create opportunities for all of their students to share their academic work—this book describes many possible tactics, such as students sharing ways they applied reading strategies they learned in school to out-of-school texts, discussing examples of writing tactics they identified outside of school, and presenting on language related to their funds of knowledge. Regardless of the specific work students are doing, I strongly recommend creating opportunities for students to share they work they've created. This doesn't need to be through a formal presentation: it can simply be a requirement that every student will share a way he or she applied a reading, writing, or language-study strategy to an out-of-school text, situation, or context.

How Can It Help Build an Inclusive Classroom?

This instructional practice can help build a student-centered classroom environment in which students have an authentic audience of their peers, which can be more meaningful to them than creating work that is only shared with a teacher (Fletcher & Portalupi, 2001). These opportunities to share with peers can also help students learn from each other while emphasizing the variety of perspectives in the classroom. For example, when the students described in Chapter 5 shared language related to their funds of knowledge with their peers, all of the students benefited: they learned about the range of their classmates' identities and experiences and developed new understandings about contexts in which specific and concrete language is important. The diversity of these perspectives, combined with the students' appreciations of these perspectives, helped build an inclusive and supportive classroom context.

Key Points about Building an Inclusive Classroom Environment

An inclusive classroom that helps all students feel safe, valued, and important is essential to culturally relevant teaching. For students to take the intellectual and personal risks associated with connecting in-school learning with important and relevant aspects of their backgrounds, communities and identities, they first need to feel like they are in a safe space with a teacher who values them as individuals and classmates who are interested in what they have to say. After my eighth graders shared examples of writing strategies they found in out-of-school texts they encountered, one student came up to me after class and noted that she felt there was a supportive environment surrounding the activity that helped her do her best work; she explained, "This activity was really fun. I think I did well because you were really supportive of us sharing examples from our home lives and connecting them to the sensory language we talked about in class. I didn't feel nervous at all. If I had felt nervous, I don't think I would have done as well."

8

Recommendations for Putting this Book's Ideas into Action

In this concluding chapter, we'll examine four key recommendations, which synthesize important points we've explored together throughout this book and are designed to help you put its ideas into action:

- Talk to students about the benefits and features of culturally relevant instruction.
- Discuss what classroom-appropriate examples are.
- Model your own relevant connections.
- Provide a clear academic focus while allowing for student ownership.

Each of these recommendations describes an important teaching tactic to utilize as you implement culturally relevant teaching practices in your instruction. By employing each of these tactics, you'll create the framework necessary for effective culturally relevant teaching. Now, let's look at each of these recommendations individually.

Talk to Students about the Benefits and Features of Culturally Relevant Instruction

I've found that an effective way to prepare students to engage in and succeed with culturally relevant teaching is to make the process transparent for them by discussing what culturally relevant teaching is and why it can be beneficial. When I do this, I begin with introductory information about what culturally relevant teaching is and how it will play a role in some of our upcoming activities. For example, before I conducted the learning activities described in this book with the fifth-, eighth-, and tenth-grade classes with which I worked, I told them that we will be doing a variety of projects that asked them to learn academic material and then connect it to information in their out-of-school lives. "We'll be studying writing strategies, reading skills, and vocabulary information," I told my fifth graders, "and then you'll look for examples of them, or ways to use them, in your out-of-school life, like song lyrics, conversations, films, books, YouTube clips, and other things you encounter outside of school. I'll help you while you do this and give you the support you need, and we'll discuss the specifics of each assignment, like what skills and strategies we'll be learning and how you can apply them to your out-of-school life, as we go along. I can't wait to see what everyone does!"

After I provide students with this initial explanation, I give an overview of the benefits of these instructional practices, describing why we'll be learning in this way: "I also want to talk to you about why we'll be doing this," I explained to this same group of fifth graders. "There are a lot of benefits that can come from applying skills and strategies you learn in school to your out-of-school lives: it can help you understand the strategies even better than if you just applied them to in-school examples, it can show you more about the importance of these skills and strategies since you'll be applying them to out-of-school situations, and it can allow all of us to learn more about our classmates' out-of-school lives, interests, and backgrounds." Sharing this information with students about the instructional practices and benefits associated with culturally relevant teaching helps make them understand what we're doing and why, which has the potential to further engage them and increase their investment in the learning activities. When I've made connections to the students' out-of-school lives without introducing the instructional goals first, students were usually engaged, but also wondered what the point of the activity was; providing students with this information at the beginning of the activity eliminates potential confusion.

Discuss What Classroom-Appropriate Examples Are

Some of the activities described in this book, such as students finding examples of writing strategies in texts they engage with outside of school and applying reading strategies to those same kinds of texts, ask students to bring excerpts of out-of-school texts into the classroom so they can share these examples and the students' analyses. Because of this, I recommend talking with your students beforehand about what language is appropriate for the classroom. While the particulars of such conversations may vary based on the age group you teach, the context of your school, and other related factors, I suggest encouraging students to bring in examples that are authentic but don't use language that can offend others. For example, I recently spoke with a tenth grader who wanted to talk about the mood in a song that contains some explicit lyrics. While the student wanted to analyze this song, he also understood that I wanted students bring in examples without explicit language that might offend other students. We looked up the lyrics to the song together and talked about excerpts from the song that depicted the mood the student identified but also used language that we agreed were appropriate for the classroom. If you encounter a similar situation in which a student wants to discuss a particular academic strategy or concept in a text that contains explicit language, I recommend employing this same tactic: talk with your student about the academic concept he or she identifies in the piece (such as an example of a writing strategy or the application of a reading strategy) and look at the text together with the student, discussing examples that the student feels represent the academic focus while still ensuring everyone can feel comfortable in the classroom.

Model Your Own Relevant Connections

To help your students connect the skills and strategies they learn in school to relevant aspects of their backgrounds, identities, interests, and out-of-school lives, I recommend demonstrating this for them by applying the strategy you're discussing with your students to a text that represents an important aspect of your out-of-school life. In this book, I describe situations in which when I've done this with my students, providing examples of how I've connected academic strategies to my out-of-school interests. For instance, when talking with my tenth graders about how authors create moods in their works through word choice, I talked about my interest in and experiences with distance running and running shoes and then shared an excerpt from website of a running shoe company, analyzing how the word choice in the excerpt creates a happy and positive mood that makes the reader feel good about running. Similarly, when talking with my students about specific vocabulary related to funds of knowledge, I talked about the importance of running-related vocabulary, such as specific events and strategies, that can help someone understand running in more detail than if that person just used general terms to describe the sport. These examples I shared with my students had multiple benefits: they provided students with models of how one might connect in-school strategies to out-of-school interests, while also sharing my passion for running (which allowed students to get to know me further and helped create an atmosphere in which out-of-school interests are celebrated and connected to learning).

Provide a Clear Academic Focus While Allowing for Student Ownership

This final recommendation addresses a key component of successful culturally relevant teaching: establish a clear academic focus for student work while also ensuring that they have ownership of the specific connections they make and examples they provide. The activities and examples described in this book will help you achieve this balance in your instruction—each chapter in the book describes one or more learning goals and discusses ways to present that academic content to students and then to help them connect that information to aspects of their out-of-school lives that they choose. Balancing academic content and student ownership helps us teachers work toward Gloria Ladson-Billings' (1995) goal, described in the book's introduction, that culturally relevant instruction uses students' cultures as vehicles for learning. A key point to keep in mind when putting culturally relevant teaching practices into action in your classroom is that we as teachers are the experts in our content areas, but students are the experts of their out-of-school lives, backgrounds, and identities. By balancing both of these important components, we can create classrooms and instructional methods that make connections between students' individual identities and the academic content they learn in school.

Final Thoughts on Culturally Relevant Teaching

I strongly believe that culturally relevant teaching is one of the most important components of effective education: it provides students with meaningful and rigorous applications of academic skills, while helping them feel valued and included in the classroom. The ideas and activities described on this book represent ways to facilitate connections between your students' out-of-school lives and the strategies they learn in school. By teaching students in culturally relevant ways, we can show them that reading, writing, and language skills aren't just useful in the classroom: they're important for all aspects of their lives.

Section 5

Resources

Appendix A
A Guide for Book Studies

Culturally Relevant Teaching in the English Language Arts Classroom is well-suited for "study groups" of teachers using the text for a book study as they explore the features of culturally relevant teaching and reflect on how to implement these practices in their own classrooms. If you are interested in discussing this text with fellow teachers who are interested in this topic, I recommend using this guide to facilitate your conversations. This guide is divided into three sections: before reading, during reading, and after reading; it contains questions and topics to consider at each of these stages. The questions in this guide are designed to help you reflect on key issues in the book and spark conversations with your colleagues about how you can apply the ideas in the book to your instruction.

Before Reading

Before beginning your experience reading and discussing *Culturally Relevant Teaching in the English Language Arts Classroom*, I recommend activating your prior knowledge of the book's central ideas by considering the following issues:

- This book focuses on helping students connect skills and strategies students learn in school to aspects of their identities, backgrounds, and out-of-school lives. What are some benefits you believe can come from connecting the skills and strategies students learn in school to their out-of-school lives and interests?
- What are some potential challenges?
- What are some academic skills you teach your students that you think can be applied to aspects of their out-of-school lives?

During Reading

In this section, I provide reflection questions and prompts to respond to after reading each of the book's chapters. These questions will help you and the other members of your study group consider important ideas and information in each chapter.

Introduction
- In the introductory chapter, I describe Gloria Ladson-Billings' (1995) assertion that culturally relevant teaching should achieve three goals: 1) Facilitate students' academic success, 2) Value students' home cultures, and 3) Help students think critically about the world around them. Why do you think it's important that culturally relevant teaching does all of these things?
- In this chapter, I also discuss Wlodkowski and Ginsberg's (1995) work on this topic that identified four reasons why culturally relevant instruction can facilitate students' success: 1) It can create an inclusive classroom, 2) It can improve students' attitudes, 3) It can make students' work more meaningful, and 4) It can increase students' feelings of competence. Pick one of these four statements and explain why culturally relevant teaching can have this benefit.

Chapter 1
- This chapter identifies three benefits of students identifying examples of writing strategies they learn in school to texts they encounter in their out-of-school lives: it can give students additional opportunities to apply their understandings of writing strategies, it can help students build confidence in their knowledge of writing strategies through the use of familiar texts, and it can show students that their cultural backgrounds and out-of-school lives belong in school. Pick one of these benefits and comment on its importance.
- What is a writing strategy you teach your students that you think they could find examples of in an out-of-school text?

Chapter 2
- One of the benefits of dialect and language variations which this chapter discusses is that it can help students think carefully and metacognitively about language use. Why do you think it's important for students to reflect on the dialect and language varieties authors use in their works?
- Consider the student work excerpts in this chapter: how do you think they are enhanced by the student authors' uses of dialect and language variations?

Chapter 3
- In this chapter, I explain that using texts that feature diverse cultures and experiences can help students see themselves reflected in the curriculum and give students opportunities to

learn about others' cultures and experiences. Why do you think it's important that students have both of these experiences?
- What are some texts featuring diverse cultures and experiences you have used or might use in the future with your students to teach them reading strategies?

Chapter 4
- This chapter discusses an instructional process that helps students apply the reading strategies they learn in school to out-of-school texts, identifying three benefits of this process: it provides students with authentic applications of academic strategies, it makes space for students' perspectives and identities, and it creates opportunities for additional uses of skills they learn in school. Pick one of these benefits and comment on its impact on students.
- Using the ideas in this chapter as a guide, how might you prepare your students to apply reading strategies they learn in school to texts that represent their out-of-school lives?

Chapter 5
- This chapter explains that incorporating students' funds of knowledge can enhance students' experiences with vocabulary instruction in two key ways: by making vocabulary instruction relevant to students' backgrounds and emphasizing the importance of specific language and vocabulary to in-depth understandings. How do you think these features can help students learn vocabulary?
- What are some funds of knowledge you feel your students possess that would lend themselves to discussions about specific language and terminology?

Chapter 6
- What are some benefits that come from students learning Greek and Latin word roots?
- How do you think connecting the study of Greek and Latin roots to words students encounter in their out-of-school lives can facilitate their understandings of those roots?

Chapter 7
- This chapter describes four tactics for building an inclusive classroom environment: 1) Incorporate diverse texts; 2) Ask students to make connections to their out-of-school lives; 3) Meet with students individually about their progress, and 4)

Sean Ruday (2019), *Culturally Relevant Teaching in the English Language Arts Classroom: A Guide for Teachers*, Routledge

Build in opportunities for all students to share. Pick one of these strategies that especially stands out to you and comment on why you think it's particularly important.

Chapter 8
- This chapter presents four key recommendations for putting culturally relevant teaching into action in your classroom: 1) Talk to students about the benefits and features of culturally relevant instruction; 2) Discuss what classroom-appropriate examples are; 3) Model your own relevant connections, and 4) Provide a clear academic focus while allowing for student ownership. Select one of these recommendations and discuss how you'll use it in your classroom.

After Reading

Now that you've completed *Culturally Relevant Teaching in the English Language Arts Classroom,* respond to these after-reading questions designed to help you synthesize the book's key ideas:

- What do you see as the most compelling reason to help students apply the skills and strategies they learn in school to their out-of-school lives, identities, and interests?
- What do you see as the greatest challenge of culturally relevant teaching?
    - How will you address this challenge?
- What is one way you will incorporate culturally relevant teaching into your classroom?

Appendix B
Reproducible Forms and Templates You Can Use in Your Classroom

Figure 1.1 Guideline Sheet for Strong Verbs and Specific Nouns in Community Conversations

Investigative Work: Strong Verbs and Specific Nouns in Community Conversations!

- In our past few classes, we've been discussing strong verbs and specific nouns. We've examined what these writing strategies are and why they're important to effective communication.
- Now, we get to put our knowledge of this strategy into action by investigating its role in the conversations we have in our communities!
- You'll do investigative work on this topic by identifying examples of strong verbs and specific you hear outside of school and reflecting on their impact.
- Use the graphic organizers below to guide your observations and analyses.

Writing Strategy	Strong verb
Example	
Context	
Why the writing strategy is important to the effectiveness of the original statement	

Writing Strategy	Specific noun
Example	
Context	
Why the writing strategy is important to the effectiveness of the original statement	

Sean Ruday (2019), *Culturally Relevant Teaching in the English Language Arts Classroom: A Guide for Teachers*, Routledge

Figure 1.2 Guideline Sheet for Identifying and Analyzing Culturally Relevant Examples of Sensory Language

---

Investigative Work: Identifying and Analyzing Sensory Language

- Recently, we've been discussing the writing strategy of sensory language; we've explored the features of this concept, examined examples of it in literature, and discussed how the use of sensory details gives the audience a clear understanding of characters' experiences and allows writers to focus on important aspects of situations.
- Today, we're taking our work with this strategy to a new level: instead of looking for examples of sensory language in literature, you're going to be identifying and analyzing how this strategy is used in real-world situations that you encounter outside of school. For example, you might notice sensory language in a song you hear, a conversation you have, a social media post or text you read, or a television show you watch.
- The graphic organizer below will help you identify and analyze examples of sensory language you encounter. It calls for you to document three examples; they can all be from the same text or different texts. The examples can relate to different senses, the same senses, or some combination (such as two examples related to the sense of sight and one to the sense of smell).

Sensory Language	
Context	
Related Sense	
How do you think the sensory language impacts the effectiveness of the text in which it is used?	

Sean Ruday (2019), *Culturally Relevant Teaching in the English Language Arts Classroom: A Guide for Teachers*, Routledge

Sensory Language	
Context	
Related Sense	
How do you think the sensory language impacts the effectiveness of the text in which it is used?	

Sensory Language	
Context	
Related Sense	
How do you think the sensory language impacts the effectiveness of the text in which it is used?	

Figure 1.3 Guideline Sheet for Identifying and Reflecting on Culturally Relevant Examples of Connotation-Rich Language

---

Investigative Work: Identifying and Reflecting on Out-of-School Examples of Connotation-Rich Language

- We've been working hard lately on the concept of connotation (the feelings and emotions associated with a word) and how it is similar to and different from denotation (the dictionary definition of a word).
- We looked at how words with similar denotations can have different connotations; for example, we discussed how "leisurely" and "lazy" both have denotations related to avoiding strenuous effort, but "leisurely" has a positive connotation and "lazy" has a negative one.
- After that, we discussed the importance of connotation to effective communication; we reflected on how this concept allows authors and speakers to ensure their audiences interpret their statements in the ways they intended.
- Now, you're going to take what you've learned about the importance of connotation and apply it to language you encounter outside of school. To do this, think about language you read and hear in your out-of-school communication. You might ask yourself questions like, "What are some connotations of the words I hear in my home and community?" "How does connotation impact language I encounter in extra-curricular activities, such as sports, arts, and clubs?" and "How is the concept of connotation important to information I encounter on social media?"
- To complete this activity, you'll identify two examples of connotation-rich language and analyze them. You'll use the graphic organizer provided, which asks you to identify connotation-rich language you encounter in out-of-school situations, note the relevant denotations and connotations, and reflect on why the connotation of the language you identified is important to the effectiveness of the larger communication context (such as the conversation, song, discussion, or text message) in which it was used.

Connotation-rich language you identified	
Context	

Sean Ruday (2019), *Culturally Relevant Teaching in the English Language Arts Classroom: A Guide for Teachers*, Routledge

Denotation	
Connotation	
Why the connotation of the language you identified is important to the effectiveness of the communication context in which it was used	

Connotation-rich language you identified	
Context	
Denotation	
Connotation	
Why the connotation of the language you identified is important to the effectiveness of the communication context in which it was used	

Sean Ruday (2019), *Culturally Relevant Teaching in the English Language Arts Classroom: A Guide for Teachers*, Routledge

Figure 2.2 Graphic Organizer for Student Identification and Analysis of Dialect and/or Informal Language

Investigative Work: Identifying and Analyzing Dialect and Informal Language

- We've been thinking lately about the importance of dialect and informal language: we looked at a published text that contains these language features and discussed why the author may have chosen to use dialect and informal language in that work.
- In this activity, you're going to apply our knowledge of this topic to the language you encounter in your out-of-school life.
- First, you'll identify an example of dialect or informal language you hear or read in your everyday life. (Some possible situations in which you might notice these language forms are conversations in which you participate, dialogue that takes place around you, interactions in films or television shows, songs you hear, text messages you receive, and communication you find on social media. There are many other possibilities as well!) Then, you'll note the context in which that language was used. Finally, you'll then reflect on why the language used was important to the effectiveness of the communication—in other words, why the speaker or author chose to use dialect and inform
- You'll do this identification and analysis twice using the graphic organizer below and the one on the next page.

Example of dialect or informal language	
Context in which it was used	

Sean Ruday (2019), *Culturally Relevant Teaching in the English Language Arts Classroom: A Guide for Teachers*, Routledge

Why the language used was important to the effectiveness of the communication	

Example of dialect or informal language	
Context in which it was used	
Why the language used was important to the effectiveness of the communication	

Figure 3.1 Making Connections Graphic Organizer

Your name:

Book you're reading:

Connection type	Connection you made	Explanation of the connection
Text-to-text		
Text-to-self		
Text-to-world		

Sean Ruday (2019), *Culturally Relevant Teaching in the English Language Arts Classroom: A Guide for Teachers*, Routledge

Figure 3.2 Inferences Graphic Organizer

Your name:

Book you're reading:

An inference you made	Textual evidence for that inference	Explanation of how the textual evidence led you to make that inference

Sean Ruday (2019), *Culturally Relevant Teaching in the English Language Arts Classroom: A Guide for Teachers*, Routledge

Figure 3.3 Mood Graphic Organizer

Your name:

Book you're reading:

Mood the author creates	Language the author uses to create the mood	Why you believe these language choices create the mood

Sean Ruday (2019), *Culturally Relevant Teaching in the English Language Arts Classroom: A Guide for Teachers*, Routledge

Figure 4.1 Graphic Organizer for Making Connections to an Out-of-School Text

Your name:

Out-of-school text you chose:

Connection type	**Connection you made**	**Explanation of the connection**
Text-to-text		
Text-to-self		
Text-to-world		

Sean Ruday (2019), *Culturally Relevant Teaching in the English Language Arts Classroom: A Guide for Teachers*, Routledge

Figure 4.2 Graphic Organizer for Creating Inferences with an Out-of-School Text

Your name:

Out-of-school text you chose:

An inference you made	Textual evidence for that inference	Explanation of how the textual evidence led you to make that inference

Sean Ruday (2019), *Culturally Relevant Teaching in the English Language Arts Classroom: A Guide for Teachers*, Routledge

Figure 4.3 Graphic Organizer for Analyzing Mood in an Out-of-School Text

Your name:

Out-of-school text you chose:

Mood created in the piece	Language used to create the mood	Why you believe these language choices create the mood

Sean Ruday (2019), *Culturally Relevant Teaching in the English Language Arts Classroom: A Guide for Teachers*, Routledge

Figure 5.1 Graphic Organizer: Funds of Knowledge and Language

Fund of Knowledge	Key Terms Related to the Fund of Knowledge and Their Meanings	Why Each Term is Important to Understanding the Topic

Sean Ruday (2019), *Culturally Relevant Teaching in the English Language Arts Classroom: A Guide for Teachers*, Routledge

Figure 6.1 Selected High-Frequency Greek and Latin-Based Word Roots

Root	Meaning	Used in a Word
Anti	Against	Antisocial
Arch	Most important	Archenemy
Biblio	Book	Bibliography
Bio	Life	Biology
Celer	Fast	Accelerate
Cert	Sure	Certain
Dem, Demo	People	Democracy
Ego	I	Egotistic
Extra, Extro	Beyond	Extraterrestrial
Geo	Related to the earth	Geology
Mal	Bad, wrongful	Malevolent
Max	Largest	Maximize
Mem	Mind	Memory
Nov	New	Novice
Omni	All	Omnivore
Path	Emotion	Empathy
Post	After	Postpone
Sol	Sun	Solar
Un	Opposite	Unfair
Ver	Truth	Verify

Sean Ruday (2019), *Culturally Relevant Teaching in the English Language Arts Classroom: A Guide for Teachers*, Routledge

Figure 6.2 Graphic Organizer for Connecting Word Roots with Students' Out-of-School Lives, Backgrounds, and Cultures

Word root	
The root's meaning	
Word you've encountered outside of school (in English or another language) that contains this root	
Where you encountered the word	
The word's meaning	
Connection between the word and the root it contains	

Sean Ruday (2019), *Culturally Relevant Teaching in the English Language Arts Classroom: A Guide for Teachers,* Routledge

Appendix C
Classroom Library Recommendations— Multicultural Texts

This section contains recommendations of multicultural texts teachers can include in their classroom libraries (or administrators and librarians can incorporate in school libraries) to ensure that a wide range of cultures and backgrounds are represented in the offerings available to their students. These text-recommendation lists are grouped in three sections: upper-elementary, middle, and high school. I focused on books that have been published relatively recently to help teachers identify current texts. Some of these works are also used as exemplars earlier in this book, while others represent additional excellent works that contain multicultural perspectives. It's important to note that the grade ranges listed here are intended to provide general guidelines on a text and are not meant to limit students. I encourage you to use to your knowledge of your students, such as their interests, skills, and maturity levels, when helping them select individual books. Of course, this list isn't intended to be inclusive of all high-quality multicultural texts; it's meant to provide some possible works to consider when incorporating diverse works into a classroom or school library.

Upper Elementary

The Crossover by Kwame Alexander (2014)
A Long Pitch Home by Natalie Dias Lorenzi (2016)
Where the Mountain Meets the Moon by Grace Lin (2009)
One Crazy Summer by Rita Williams-Garcia (2010)
Brown Girl Dreaming by Jacqueline Woodson (2014)

Middle School

The Absolutely True Diary of a Part-Time Indian by Sherman Alexie (2007)
Amina's Voice by Hena Khan (2017)
Amal Unbound by Aisha Saeed (2018)
The Epic Fail of Arturo Zamora by Pablo Cartaya (2017)
Piecing Me Together by Renee Watson (2017)

High School

The Hate U Give by Angie Thomas (2017)
All-American Boys by Jason Reynolds and Brandon Kiely (2015)
I Am Not Your Perfect Mexican Daughter by Erika L. Sanchez (2017)
American Street by Ibi Zoboi (2017)
The Poet X by Elizabeth Acevedo (2018)

Appendix D
Recommendations for Parent Communication

Communicating with parents about the features and benefits of these instructional methods can ensure that they understand what culturally relevant teaching is and how it can enhance students' learning experiences. Sharing this information with parents can help establish a supportive relationship between you and them, in which they understand what you're doing in the classroom, why you're doing it, and how they can help their students be successful. In this section, I describe three recommendations for communicating with students' parents and guardians about culturally relevant English language arts instruction.

My first recommendation for communicating with parents about culturally relevant teaching is to send home information at the beginning of implementing these instructional practices that describe what students will be doing and why. To do this, you can send parents a letter or email discussing the features and benefits of culturally relevant teaching, include the information in a class newsletter, or post information about it on a class website and direct parents to the site. By sharing this information early in the process, you can ensure that parents have clear understandings of what culturally relevant teaching is, thereby reducing the chances of parents emailing or calling you to express confusion. When I began implementing culturally relevant instruction with the elementary-, middle-, and high-school classes described in this book, I sent home a letter to the parents and guardians of the students in each of these classes. In the letter, I explained, "The students will be learning key skills and strategies essential to effective writing, reading, and vocabulary usage. Once they learn what these strategies are and understand their significance, they will identify examples of these concepts in their out-of-school lives (such as their cultures, backgrounds, and interests), analyze why the concepts are important to the out-of-school examples they identified, and share their examples and analyses with the class. This instructional method has been shown to increase students' engagement levels and understandings of the importance of the academic skills and strategies they learn."

My second recommendation is to invite parents to come and watch a class in which you and the students discuss literacy strategies and their connections to students' out-of-school lives. I like to extend this invitation twice: first as a general offer in my initial letter about culturally relevant teaching, explaining that the parents are more than welcome to come see a class and experience this instruction firsthand, and then again before specific classes that I feel provide excellent insights into the benefits of culturally relevant teaching. For example, I invited my students' parents to come to class on days when I was modeling a certain strategy that I thought conveyed the benefits and features of culturally relevant teaching and on days when students would be sharing their identifications and analyses of how they applied the reading, writing, and language-study strategies they learned to their out-of-school lives. These invitations helped parents feel included in the classroom and allowed them to see firsthand what culturally relevant teaching looks like.

My third recommendation is to tell parents and guardians how they can contribute to their students' culturally relevant learning: parents and other family members can be excellent resources for students trying to connect academic strategies to aspects of their out-of-school lives. For example, parents can help as children identify vocabulary related to their cultural backgrounds, discuss examples of dialect related to the family's experiences, find examples of writing strategies in descriptions of family and cultural traditions, and apply reading strategies to songs, stories, and shows that the family has experienced together. I communicated this opportunity to my students' parents when I wrote to introduce them to culturally relevant teaching: "This method of instruction provides great opportunities for families to be involved in what students are learning. Since students will be connecting the strategies they learn in school with meaningful information in their out-of-school lives, they may want to talk further with you about your family's background, traditions, and experiences."

As we've discussed throughout this book, culturally relevant teaching provides students with many academic and personal benefits; it can be even more effective when parents and families are involved and supportive. These recommendations can help establish the foundation of parent support that can maximize the impact of the culturally relevant instruction you provide your students.

References

Acevedo, E. (2018). *The poet X*. New York, NY: HarperTeen.

Alexander, K. (2014). *The crossover*. New York, NY: Houghton Mifflin Harcourt.

Alexie, S. (2007). *The absolutely true diary of a part-time Indian*. New York, NY: Little, Brown and Company.

Anderson, D.K. (Producer), Unkrich, L., & Molina, A. (Directors). (2017). *Coco* [Motion picture]. United States: Disney Pixar.

Azano, A. (2011). The possibility of place: One teacher's use of place-based instruction for English students in a rural high school. *Journal of Research in Rural Education*, 26 (10), 1–12.

Barris, K. (Producer). (2018). *Blackish* [Television series]. Hollywood, CA: American Broadcasting Company.

Baskin, B. (2018). Face of the NFL? Saquon Barkley has a plan. *Sports Illustrated*. Retrieved from: https://www.si.com/nfl/2018/04/18/saquon-barkley-2018-nfl-draft

Bishop, R. S. (1990). Mirrors, windows, and sliding glass doors. *Perspectives: Choosing and Using Books for the Classroom*, 6(3), ix–xi.

Brooks Running. (2018). *Our beliefs*. Retrieved from http://www.brooksrunning.com/en_us/our-beliefs.html

Cartaya, P. (2017). *The epic fail of Arturo Zamora*. New York, NY: Puffin Books.

Commemorative [Def 1]. (n.d.). *Merriam Webster Online*. Retrieved from https://www.merriam-webster.com/dictionary/commemorative

Common Core State Standards Initiative (2010). Common core state standards for English language arts. Retrieved from http://www.corestandards.org

Dahl, R. (1970). *Fantastic Mr. Fox*. New York, NY: Puffin Books.

Duncan-Andrade, J., & Morrell, E. (2005). Turn up that radio, teacher: Popular cultural pedagogy in new century urban schools. *Journal of School Leadership,* 15 (3), 284–304.

DuPrau, J. (2003). *The city of ember*. New York, NY: Yearling.

Feige, K. (Producer), & Coogler, R. (Director). (2018). *Black panther*. [Motion picture]. Hollywood, CA: Disney.

Ferlazzo, L. (2015). *Building a community of self-motivated learners: Strategies to help students thrive in school and beyond*. New York, NY: Routledge Eye on Education.

Fitzgerald, F.S. (1925). *The great Gatsby*. New York, NY: Charles Scribner's Sons.

Fleischman, P. (2004). *Seedfolks*. New York, NY: HarperTrophy.

Fletcher, R., & Portalupi, J. (2001). *Writing workshop: The essential guide*. Portsmouth, NH: Heinemann.

Garza, C.L. (1990). *Family pictures/Cuadros de familia*. San Francisco, CA: Children's Book Press.

Gonzalez, N., Moll, L.C., & Amanti, C. (Eds.) (2005). *Funds of knowledge: Theorizing practices in households, communities, and classrooms*. New York, NY: Routledge.

Gratz, A. (2017). *Refugee*. New York, NY: Scholastic.

Green, M.A. (2017). LeBron James is the greatest living athlete (and here's why). *GQ*. Retrieved from https://www.gq.com/story/lebron-james-greatest-living-athlete

Grimes, N. (2002). *Bronx masquerade*. New York, NY: Dial Books.

Howard, T. (2001). Telling their side of the story: African-American students' perceptions of culturally relevant teaching. *The Urban Review*, 33 (2), 131–149.

Katz, J. (2016). *Speaking American: How y'all, youse, and you guys talk*. New York, NY: Houghton Mifflin Harcourt.

Khan, H. (2017). *Amina's voice*. New York, NY: Salaam Reads.

Kolln, M., & Funk, R. (2012). *Understanding English grammar* (9th ed.). New York, NY: Pearson.

Kumar, R., Zusho, A., & Bondie, R. (2018). Weaving cultural relevance and achievement motivation into inclusive classroom cultures. *Educational Psychologist*, 53 (2), 78–96.

Ladson-Billings, G. (1995). But that's just good teaching! The case for culturally relevant pedagogy. *Theory into Practice*, 34 (3), 159–165.

Lin, G. (2009). *Where the mountain meets the moon*. New York, NY: Little, Brown Books for Young Readers.

Lorenzi, N. D. (2016). *A long pitch home*. Watertown, MA: Charlesbridge.

Mims, C. (2003). Authentic learning: A practical introduction and guide for implementation. *Meridian: A Middle School Computer Technologies Journal*, 6, (1), n.p. Retrieved from https://projects.ncsu.edu/meridian/win2003/authentic_learning/index.html

Moll, L.C., & Greenberg, J. (1990). Creating zones of possibilities: Combining social contexts for instruction. In L.C. Moll (Ed.), *Vygotsky and education* (pp. 319–348). New York, NY: Cambridge University Press.

Myers, W.D. (2000). "Block party—145th Street style." In W.D. Myers, *145th Street: Short stories* (pp.139–151). New York, NY: Random House.

National Council of Teachers of English. (2003). Resolution on affirming the CCCC "Students' Right to Their Own Language." Retrieved from http://www2.ncte.org/statement/affirmingstudents

Padak, N., Newton, E., Rasinski, T., & Newton, R.M. (2008). Getting to the root of word study: Teaching Latin and Greek word roots in elementary and middle grades. In A. E. Farstrup & S. J. Samuels (Eds.), *What research has to say about vocabulary instruction* (pp. 6–31). Newark, DE: International Reading Association.

Palacio, R.J. (2012). *Wonder*. New York, NY: Alfred A. Knopf.
Philbrick, R. (1993). *Freak the mighty*. New York, NY: Scholastic.
Rasinski, T., Padak, N., & Newton, J. (2017). The roots of comprehension. *Educational Leadership*, 74 (5), 41–45.
Reynolds, J. (2017). *Patina*. New York, NY: Atheneum Books for Young Readers.
Reynolds, J., & Kiely, B. (2015). *All-American boys*. New York, NY: Atheneum Books for Young Readers.
Ruday, S. (2016). *The narrative writing toolkit: Using mentor texts in grades 3–8*. New York, NY: Routledge Eye on Education.
Saeed, A. (2018). *Amal unbound*. New York, NY: Penguin Random House.
Sanchez, E. L. *I am not your perfect Mexican daughter*. (2017). New York, NY: Alfred A. Knopf.
Sitomer, A.L. (2006). *Hip-hop high school*. New York, NY: Hyperion.
Souto-Manning, M., & Martell, J. (2016). *Reading, writing, and talk: Inclusive strategies for teaching diverse learners, K-2*. New York, NY: Teachers College Press.
Spencer, C. (Producer), & Howard, B. & Moore, R. (Directors). (2016). *Zootopia*. [Motion picture]. United States: Disney.
Thomas, A. (2017). *The hate u give*. New York, NY: Balzer and Bray.
Thomas, E.E. (2018). Q & A with Ebony Elizabeth Thomas: Why children need more diverse books. *Penn GSE Newsroom*. Retrieved from https://www.gse.upenn.edu/news/ebony-elizabeth-thomas-diverse-books-children
Tolmach, M. (Producer), & Kasdan, J. (Director). (2017). *Jumanji: Welcome to the jungle*. [Motion picture]. Hollywood, CA: Sony.
Tremmel, R. (2006). Changing the way we think in English education: A conversation in the universal barbershop. *English Education*, 39 (1), 10–45.
Tschida, C.M., Ryan, C.L., & Ticknor, A.S. (2014). Building on windows and mirrors: Encouraging the disruption of "single stories" through children's literature. *Journal of Children's Literature*, 40 (1), 28–39.
Watson, R. (2017). *Piecing me together*. New York, NY: Bloomsbury.
Wheeler, R., & Swords, R. (2006). *Code-switching: Teaching standard English in urban classrooms*. Urbana, IL: National Council of Teachers of English.
Williams-Garcia, R. (2010). *One crazy summer*. New York, NY: HarperCollins.
Winn, M.T., & Johnson, L. (2011). *Writing instruction in the culturally relevant classroom*. Urbana, IL: National Council of Teachers of English.
Wlodkowski, R., & Ginsberg, M. (1995). A framework for culturally responsive teaching. *Educational Leadership*, 53 (1), 17–21.
Woodson, J. (2014). *Brown girl dreaming*. New York, NY: Puffin Books.
Zoboi, I. (2017). *American street*. New York, NY: Balzer + Bray.

For Product Safety Concerns and Information please contact our EU
representative GPSR@taylorandfrancis.com
Taylor & Francis Verlag GmbH, Kaufingerstraße 24, 80331 München, Germany

www.ingramcontent.com/pod-product-compliance
Lightning Source LLC
Chambersburg PA
CBHW080938300426
44115CB00017B/2875